GEORGIA HISTORICAL MARKERS
Coastal Counties

GEORGIA HISTORICAL MARKERS
Coastal Counties

The complete text and location of the various state and non-state historical markers located throughout Bryan, Camden, Chatham, Glynn, Liberty, and McIntosh Counties.

Over 100 Photographs and Illustrations

Kenneth W. Boyd

Savannah
Tybee Island
Richmond Hill
Sunbury
Midway
Hinesville
Riceboro
Darien
St. Simons Island
Brunswick
Jekyll Island
Woodbine
Kingsland
St. Marys

Cherokee Publishing Company
Atlanta, Georgia
1991

Library of Congress Cataloging-in-Publication Data

Boyd, Kenneth W., 1938-
    Georgia historical markers / Kenneth W. Boyd. — 1st edition
        p.   cm.
    Includes indexes.
    Contents : [1] Metro Atlanta counties — [2] Coastal counties.
    ISBN 0-87797-216-8 (v. 1 : trade paper : acid-free paper) : $9.95.
    ISBN 0-87797-215-X (v. 2 : trade paper : acid-free paper) : $9.95
    1. Historical markers—Georgia—Atlanta Region—Guide-books.
2. Atlanta Region (Ga.)—History, Local.   3. Atlanta Region (Ga.)—Description and Travel—Guide-books.   I. Title.
F294.A865A23   1991
917.58'231—dc20   90-25003
                                                                    CIP

Copyright © 1991 by Kenneth W. Boyd

This book is printed on acid-free paper which conforms to the American National Standard
Z39.48-1984 Permanence of Paper for Printed Library Materials. Paper that conforms to this
standard's requirements for pH, alkaline reserve and freedom from groundwood is anticipated to
last several hundred years without significant deterioration under normal library use and storage
conditions. ∞

Manufactured in the United States of America

First Edition

ISBN: 0-87797-215-X

98   97   96   95   94   93   92   91   10   9   8   7   6   5   4   3   2   1

Front Cover photo: Carroll Proctor Scruggs
Back Cover photos: Sir James Wright, courtesy, Georgia Department of Archives and History;
Juliette Gordon Low, Portrait by Edward Hughes,
courtesy, The National Portrait Gallery, Smithsonian Institution

Index by Alexa Selph

Design by Penny Bernath

Cherokee Publishing Company
P O Box 1730, Marietta, Georgia, 30061-1730

Dedicated
to
Wade Julius Boyd
whose roots run deep
into the red clay of Georgia

CONTENTS

SYMBOLS AND ABBREVIATIONS

◆	Marker was missing when surveyed
★	Marker not photographed or compared with printed text
Not Standing	Marker replacement is not likely
ASAE	American Society of Agricultural Engineers
ACH	Atlantic Coastal Highway Commission
BTC	Bartram Trail Conference
BOE	Board of Public Education of the City of Savannah and the County of Chatham
DAC	Daughters of the American Colonists
DAR	Daughters of the American Revolution
FWMC	Factors Walk Military Commission
GCG	Garden Club of Georgia, Inc.
GHM	Georgia Historical Commission/Department of Natural Resources
GHS/HSF	Georgia Historical Society/Historic Savannah Foundation
GHR	Georgia House Resolution
GMS	Georgia Medical Society
GLG	Grand Lodge of Georgia
HCTF	Hebrew Cemetery Trust Fund
JI/SPA	Jekyll Island/State Park Authority
MHS	Methodists Heritage Society
SVG	Savannah Volunteer Guards
TGC	Trustees Garden Club
UMC	United Methodist Church
WPA	Works Progress Administration

INTRODUCTION

Georgia's coastal islands had been the hunting and fishing grounds of the native Indians for centuries before the Europeans arrived. Claimed by Spain, a number of missions were built along the coast in an attempt to civilize and Christianize the local Indians. The missions had been abandoned for many years before the English came, but Spain still claimed the area. Fort King George (Darien) was built as a buffer between the Spaniards and their Indian allies by the colony in South Carolina before the English established Savannah.

In the eighteenth century, Edward Teach, better known as Blackbeard the Pirate, plundered ships along the coast and supposedly hid much of his gold on the golden isles. His heavy black beard is said to have been filthy and matted and tied with tiny bows. His hair was braided and he would stick slow-burning ropes into the braids to terrify his victims.

As the coastal areas were settled, vast plantations were developed for the cultivation of rice and sugar cane with the intensive labor supplied by slaves. Large quantities of timber were cut and shipped around the world. The live oak timbers to build "Old Ironsides" were cut on St. Simons Island. Louis LeConte, in the early 1800s, received frequent visitors to his world-famous botanical gardens near Riceboro.

Liberty County is rich in Colonial history, producing two of Georgia's signers of the Declaration of Independence. There are forts aplenty–Fort Frederica was built to protect the colonists from the Spanish soldiers. Fort Morris defended our new liberty from the British. And, near Fort McAllister, at very low tide, you can sometimes see a small portion of the ruins of the CSS *Rattlesnake* protruding from the Great Ogeechee River.

In 1886, after a worldwide search for a private vacation spot, a group of America's wealthiest men formed the exclusive Jekyll Island Club. Members would arrive by private railroad cars in Brunswick or by private yacht at the Club. The Club season was usually from after New Year's until just before Easter.

The blend of old and new along the Georgia coast may perhaps best be shown by the ruins of the tabby Sugar Works built in 1825, standing just outside the entrance to the Navy's nuclear submarine base near St. Marys.

HAS ANYONE SEEN THE BACON?

As a youngster growing up in Savannah, I was surrounded by monuments, historical markers, statues, plaques, historic buildings, city squares, iron railings, live oak trees, azaleas, and Spanish moss. There was no way to escape being enveloped by the remnants of and memorials to Georgia's early history. From my first visit to the Pirates' House (it became a restaurant in 1954) with its secret passage to the river, to wondering what was behind the wall at Wormsloe (not open to the public at that time), to exploring Factor's Walk – I never questioned that Savannah was a unique and special place. As a boy, I would follow the local custom of walking up to Tomo-chi-chi's boulder and asking what he was doing. "Nothing," was the usual reply.

As I became acquainted with the historical markers in my hometown, I learned that the cotton gin was invented near Savannah, and that in its heyday, Savannah was the second busiest seaport in the world for the export of cotton. Robert E. Lee's first military assignment was at Fort Pulaski, and Juliette Gordon Low founded the Girl Scouts of America at Savannah in 1912. John Wesley founded Methodism here; Conrad Aiken, the Pulitzer Prize–winning poet, was born, died, and is buried in Savannah; and "Jingle Bells" was supposedly written here. The first steamship to cross the Atlantic Ocean departed Savannah on May 22, 1819. As for the bacon, it was consumed as fuel in the furnaces of two Confederate gunboats while they were desperately escaping up the Savannah River from the fire of Federal shore batteries.

I hope you come to share my fascination with the coastal counties of Georgia, and with their history as told through the text of historical markers.

ORGANIZATION OF MATERIAL

The marker texts are arranged alphabetically by county and then by city. Within a city, the texts are arranged in a logical geographic sequence. Markers physically standing side by side or close to each other on the street will have their texts next to or close to each other in the book.

METHODS USED TO COMPILE INFORMATION

We have attempted to identify, accurately record the text, and provide the locations, of hundreds of roadside historical markers. Most markers have been located and photographed to ensure that the text in the book accurately records the text on the marker itself. We have not attempted to edit or make corrections to the marker text – in fact, we have diligently attempted to record the text exactly as it appears on the marker. We *have* tucked a number of periods and commas inside quotation marks, and obvious or known inaccuracies in the text have usually been noted. Differences and variations in spellings, capitalizations, or dates have not been tampered with. The errors that remain or those that have been freshly created are solely the responsibility of the compiler.

We have attempted to provide the location of each marker with directions specific enough so that they may be located with relative ease. Distances were usually measured from the local courthouse or post office. If a marker was not present when our survey was made, it is noted by a ♦. If we were unable to photograph a marker, and therefore unable to verify the text, it is noted by a ★. Occasionally we could photograph a marker while it was in the maintenance shop. If a marker is not likely to reappear or be replaced, it is noted by "**not standing**." The lack of replacement is usually because the sponsoring organization is not active, although some markers have been intentionally removed or discarded. The organization responsible for erecting the marker and the date of erection, when known, are also noted. Please refer to the list of abbreviations to determine the correct identity of each sponsor.

Since most markers were erected many years ago, lakes have been developed, new roads built, old roads forgotten or blocked off, street names have changed, and many highway route numbers are different. It is likely that there are markers standing that we failed to discover. If you have knowledge of markers (metal markers mounted on a post) not included in this work, please write us at Cherokee Publishing Company, P O Box 1730, Marietta, GA 30061-1730, giving us a description, location, and, if possible, a photo, of the marker text. If you locate a marker with incomplete or inaccurate directions, we would appreciate your forwarding that information to us.

SCOPE AND CRITERIA

This work is a partial, but major revision of the earlier book *Georgia Historical Markers* (1973) by Carroll Proctor Scruggs. The earlier book included only markers erected by the Georgia Historical Commission and the Georgia Department of Natural Resources. This work has been expanded to include the markers erected by the Atlantic Coastal Highway Commission, the Daughters of the American Colonists, the Daughters of the American Revolution, the Garden Club of Georgia, Inc., the Grand Lodge of Georgia, the Works Progress Administration, and a number of independent organizations including a few markers of unknown sponsorship. Plaques, monuments, and statues have been excluded. With few exceptions, only metal historical markers mounted on a post have been included.

DESCRIPTION OF HISTORIC MARKER PROGRAMS IN GEORGIA

Georgia's Official Historical Marker Program was begun when the Georgia Historical Commission was established in 1951 and continues today under the guidance of the Parks, Recreation and Historic Sites Division of the Department of Natural Resources. The first markers were erected in 1952.

Georgia was the thirteenth and last British colony and one of the thirteen original states. Its history is intimately involved with Indians, colonists, missionaries, traders, goldminers, and the military forces of Great Britain, France, and Spain. Among the purposes of historical marker programs is simple recognition, which serves to identify and encourage the preservation of the wealth of historical resources in Georgia. Markers are an effective way to inform both residents and visitors alike about significant places, events, and people in Georgia's past. Some markers, these "tombstones on posts," will remind us that our liberty is worth fighting and dying for and will remind us of the tremendous sacrifices made by those who passed before. Some places identified by markers contain tangible reminders of the past, such as an old mill, fort, or cemetery. Other markers simply mark the spot where such a structure once stood, or they mark the location of historical events that have unfolded.

There is a heavy concentration of markers relating to the movements of General Sherman through Georgia – after all, many of the structures he passed were burned to the ground. Georgia is probably second in the nation in the number of officially erected markers, with only Texas having more, and Kentucky and Virginia close behind. Fulton County (Atlanta) alone has over 200 markers, which is more than in many states. Chatham County (Savannah) has over 100 markers. Markers can be found on courthouse lawns, mountaintops and front lawns, in parks and cemeteries, along major highways, and even on dirt roads.

Generally, the texts for early historical markers were prepared in the office of the Georgia Historical Commission or by the official county historian, without specific judgment criteria. Markers dealing with the Civil War were written and located under contract by two Civil War historians, Wilbur G. Kurtz, Sr., and Colonel Allen P. Julian. Currently, markers may be erected to *persons* who have been dead for at least twenty years and who made a significant impact on Georgia history; *events* that changed the course of Georgia history; *buildings* where the person who made history lived or where the event that changed history occurred; or *places* where Georgia history was made. Today new marker applications are usually initiated by interested citizens, who provide the necessary documentation. A board of reviewers then judges the application against the criteria. Usually only a few applications are approved, because most are judged to be of primarily local significance rather than of statewide or national significance. Such things as balanced and comprehensive coverage of the state, popular appeal, and safety for the marker and reader are also considered. Both new and replacement markers are subject to the same review process.

Many unofficial but historically significant markers have been erected by other organizations. The Atlantic Coastal Highway Commission erected twenty-five markers, of which five remain standing, along the Coastal Highway (U.S. 17/GA. 25) during 1930. The Garden Club of Georgia, Inc., has erected a number of Blue Star Memorial Highway markers and markers that trace the travels of naturalist William Bartram. The Works Progress Administration had a very active marker program during the Depression. The Daughters of the American Colonists, the Daughters of the American Revolution, and the Grand Lodge of Georgia have also erected a number of markers.

MARKER IDENTIFICATION, MAINTENANCE, AND RESTORATION

Historical markers are constant targets of vandals, thieves, motor vehicles, and road equipment. Additional markers are added to the "missing list" each year. It now costs the taxpayer about $1,300 to replace a missing or stolen marker. If you know of stolen, lost or damaged markers, please share your knowledge with someone at the nearest state park or historic site. You may also inform the Parks, Recreation and Historic Sites Division, Georgia Department of Natural Resources, Twin Towers East #1352, 205 Butler Street, SE, Atlanta, GA 30334. Telephone: 404-656-2770.

The state also maintains a marker repair and restoration shop at Panola Mountain Conservation Park near Atlanta. Ken Carlsrud has become an accomplished artist at bullet-hole patching, reconstruction of letters and arrows, and meticulous gold lettering and painting. Each year the shop can repair or refurbish about 130 markers. Historic Marker Shop, Panola Mountain Conservation Park, 2600 GA Highway 155, Stockbridge, GA. 30281. Telephone: 404-389-7810.

Official Georgia historical markers are easily recognized by their green color with gold lettering and the Georgia State Seal located on top. Each marker has a message space that measures 38 inches by 42 inches. Markers erected by the state usually have a numerical designation in the lower left-hand corner. For example, marker 25-62 indicates Chatham County, the 25th county alphabetically and the 62nd marker erected. The year of erection or replacement is usually found in the lower right-hand corner. Non-state markers may or may not have numerical designations, and we have therefore arbitrarily assigned many numbers in the book as a means of identification.

ACKNOWLEDGMENTS

This compiler is deeply appreciative for the assistance that many, many people gave in the gathering of this material. For several years, without success, we had attempted to locate a source giving the text of the Atlantic Coastal Highway Commission markers that were erected in 1930. At the time, we had only a general idea as to the number of markers erected and no information on the texts or locations. William Rosier of Midway, Georgia, was able to locate the texts of the twenty-five markers in a Savannah newspaper article published during 1930. Of the five markers left standing (that we know about), the newspaper text was accurate for four.

We would also like to thank Gail Miller of the Georgia Department of Archives and History and Jan Flores and Eileen Ielmini of the Georgia Historical Society Library. Also Judy Nichols of the Savannah Public Library, Kent Cave of Fort Pulaski National Monument, Billy Butler of Darien, Georgia, Elliott Edwards and Milton Rahn of Savannah, Stephen Davis of the National Girl Scout Headquarters, and Daniel Brown of Fort McAllister Historic Site.

David Seibert, a marker "nut" just like the compiler, has graciously compared our text with his own notes and records. As a fortunate result, there are fewer errors in this book.

There are several people without whose patience, assistance, interest, cooperation, and encouragement this book simply would never have been published. They are Billy Townsend, Ed Reed, and Kenneth Thomas of the Georgia Parks, Recreation and Historic Sites Division, Kenneth Carlsrud, and the late Al Ewing of the Historical Marker Maintenance Shop section. Thank You!

COLONIAL GEORGIA

Ceded
Lands

St Paul
Parish   • Augusta

St George
Parish

St Matthew Parish

St Philip Parish

St John
Parish   Savannah
                                              Christ
              Midway   Church
                                              Parish

St Andrew Parish   Sunbury
                                     St Catherines
St David Parish   Island

St Patrick Parish   Darien

St James Parish

St Thomas Parish

St Mary Parish

BRYAN.COUNTY

Named in honor of Jonathan Bryan (1708-1788) who came from South Carolina with General James Oglethorpe to help establish the Georgia colony at Savannah. County Seat: Pembroke.

BLITCHTON

OLD RIVER ROAD

The highway running north is the Old River Road, one of the earliest routes west of the Ogeechee and a leading way from Savannah to Georgia's western frontier. It followed the course of an Indian trail along the Ogeechee to a point west of Bartow, thence to the Rock Landing on the Oconee River, below Milledgeville. There the trace intersected the main strand of the Lower Creek Trading Path from Augusta to the Creek Indians of western Georgia and eastern Alabama. Opening of this part of the old road was authorized by the State in 1777. In time the route became an important vehicular thoroughfare from Savannah to Milledgeville.

(Located at the junction of US 80 and US 280. GHM 015-5B, 1957.)
♦ ★

JENCKS BRIDGE

On Nov. 15, 1864, after destroying Atlanta and cutting his communications with the North, Maj. Gen. W. T. Sherman, USA, began his destructive Campaign for Savannah – the March to the Sea. He divided his army (U) into two wings. The Left Wing (14th and 20th Corps), Maj. Gen. H. W. Slocum, USA, moved east from Atlanta in two columns which converged on Milledgeville, crossed the Ogeechee River near Louisville, then marched toward Savannah by two routes: the 14th Corps (Davis) on the old road near the Savannah River (Ga 24), the 20th Corps (Williams) via Springfield. Both corps approached Savannah via Monteith. Gen. Sherman accompanied the Left Wing as far as Sandersville.

The Right Wing (15th and 17th Corps), Maj. Gen. O. O. Howard, USA, marched south via Gordon and crossed the Oconee River at Ball's Ferry. The 17th Corps (Blair) moved on roads south of the Central Railroad until opposite Midville, crossed the Ogeechee River there, and moved via Millen and Eden, destroying the railroad enroute. Gen. Sherman accompanied the 17th Corps from Tennille to the outskirts of Savannah.

The 15th Corps, Maj. Gen. P. J. Osterhaus, USA, moved in two columns, the right via Statesboro, reaching the Ogeechee River here at Jencks Bridge on Dec. 6th. Finding the bridge burned, a pontoon bridge was laid. Rice's brigade crossed, drove back the defenders (C) with minor losses, and moved on Eden to join Woods' brigade, which had crossed 3 miles upstream at Wright's Bridge.

(Located on US 80 East/GA 26 at the Ogeechee River bridge. GHM 015-10, 1963.) **Note:** Variation – both Jencks and Jenk's are used.

SHERMAN'S RIGHT WING

On Dec. 6, 1864, the 15th Corps (U), the extreme right of Gen. Sherman's army on its destructive March to the Sea, camped near Jenk's Bridge on Great Ogeechee River, east of Blitchton. On the 7th, Oliver's brigade was sent in advance of Hazen's division to seize the bridge over Canoochee River east of Bryan Court House (Clyde). Beginning at Black Creek, his advance was resisted by Confederate cavalry. After continual skirmishing, Oliver's superior force reached the bridge only to find it in flames and the crossing strongly defended. Unable to advance, he returned to Bryan Court House to await Hazen's arrival.

(Located on US 280/GA 30 at Black Creek Church Road, 3.6 miles West of junction with US 80. GHM 015-11, 1959.) **Note:** Variation – both Jencks and Jenk's are used.

PEMBROKE

BRYAN COUNTY

This county created by Act of the Legislature Dec. 19, 1793, is named for Jonathan Bryan, Revolutionary patriot and member of the Executive Council in 1777. The "lost town" of Hardwick on the Ogeechee River was the first temporary County Site. Laid out in 1755, it was named for Lord Hardwick, Lord Chancellor of England, a relative of the then Gov. Reynolds. Two Royal Governors recommended that it be the Capital of Georgia. An Act of 1797 designated a new County Site at Cross Roads, 2 miles from Ogeechee Bridge. The site was later moved to Clyde and then Pembroke.

(Located on College Street, on the court house lawn. GHM 015-1, 1954.)

RICHMOND HILL

FORT McALLISTER – 10 MI.

Situated at Genesis Point, 10 miles east on the right bank of the Great Ogeechee River below the "lost town" of Hardwick, this fort was the right of the exterior line designed for the defense of Savannah. It denied the use of the river to Union vessels, protected King's Bridge (2.5 miles north) and the Savannah and Gulf (ACL) RR bridge 2 miles below, and preserved the river plantations from Union raids. Built 1861-62 to guard the "back door" to Savannah, during 1862-63 it repulsed with minor losses

CARROLL PROCTOR SCRUGGS

FORT MCALLISTER

seven attacks by armored vessels, some mounting 15-inch guns.

Fort McAllister finally fell on Dec. 13, 1864, when attacked from the rear by Hazen's Division, 15th Corps (U), which passed this point about 7 A.M. and marched via Bryan Neck road (Ga 63). Although its commander, Major George W. Anderson, refused to surrender, all resistance was smothered under waves of Union infantry which the small garrison of 230 officers and men could not long resist. The fall of Fort McAllister opened the Great Ogeechee River to Union supply ships and enabled Gen. Sherman to establish a base at King's Bridge. From it, he could supply his whole army (about 60,000 men) which, after a 300 mile march from Atlanta, was then closing in on Savannah.

(Located on US 17/GA 25 at junction with GA 144. GHM 015-6, 1957.)

"DEAD TOWN" OF HARDWICKE – 8 MI.

On May 10, 1754, GEORGE TOWN was established at the "Elbow" of Great Ogeechee River, eight miles east. In February, 1755, Gov. Reynolds, dissatisfied with Savannah as a capital and as a port, chose this new site because it "has a charming situation, the winding of the river making it a peninsula; and it is the only fit place for the capital." He preferred the deeper channel, the less lofty bluff, the more central location in the province, and the greater distance from the rival port of Charleston. He renamed it

HARDWICKE in honor of his kinsman, the Earl of Hardwicke, Lord High Chancellor of England. Lots sold quickly, the plan's backers were granted 21,000 acres of land, and fortifications were planned; but the Home Government granted no funds and the project died, dooming Hardwicke (later HARDWICK) to obscurity.

In 1758, Hardwicke was included in the newly created Parish of St. Philip. In 1793, Bryan County was created, with Hardwicke as County Site. In 1797, the County Site was removed to "Cross Roads" (Richmond Hill). By 1824, Alexander Netherclift was the sole resident. In 1866, an attempt was made to revive HARDWICK, but it failed; and so the town which might have become one of its capitals became, instead, one of the "dead towns" of Georgia.

(Located on US 17/GA 25 at junction with GA 144. GHM 015-8, 1957.)

ON THIS BANK
OF OGEECHEE RIVER

October 1, 1779. Colonel John E. White and six men by strategy forced surrender of British force of 111 regular troops and five armed vessels.

(Located on US 17. ACH 015-90, 1930.) ♦ ★ – not standing.

FORT McALLISTER – 1864

Nine miles east are ruins of Fort McAllister., several times attacked by the Federal gunboats. On December 13, 1864, was surrendered by Major Geo. W. Anderson to troops of General Sherman.

(Located on US 17. ACH 015-91, 1930.) ♦ ★ – not standing.

LOST TOWN OF
HARDWICK – 1755

Seven miles east, site of Hardwick. Reynolds, First Royal Governor, selected it, 1755, for new Capital, intending to abandon Savannah. De Brahm, Crown Surveyor, drew plans. Project failed.

(Located on US 17. ACH 015-92, 1930.) ♦ ★ – not standing.

HAZEN'S DIVISION
AT THE CANOOCHEE RIVER

On Dec. 6, 1864, the 15th Corps (U), Maj. Gen. P. J. Osterhaus, USA, the extreme right of Gen. Sherman's army on its destructive March to the Sea, camped near Jenk's Bridge on Great Ogeechee River east of Blitchton. On the 7th, Oliver's brigade of Hazen's division was sent down the west bank of the Ogeechee to seize the bridge over Canoochee River, two miles southeast of Bryan Court House (Eden) (Clyde) and one-half mile northwest of this point. From Black Creek to the Canoochee, the advance was resisted by Confederate cavalry.

After skirmishing most of the way, Oliver reached the bridge only to find it in flames and the south bank held by infantry and artillery (C) under Col. John C. Fizer. The position being naturally strong, with swamps along the river, Oliver withdrew to Bryan Court House to await Hazen's arrival.

On the 8th, Hazen reached Bryan Court House accompanied by Gen. Osterhaus and supported by Wood's division, which was posted near Fort Argyle on the Ogeechee. Learning of an abandoned ferry site downstream from the bridge, Hazen sent a party across during the night, flanked the position at the bridge, and forced the defenders to fall back toward "Cross Roads" (Richmond Hill). At dawn, the bridge was repaired and two brigades crossed. One moved to Station No. 2 (Way's), the other to Station No. 3 (Fleming), to break the Savannah and Gulf (ACL) Railroad at those points.

(Located on GA 144, 4.2 miles west of junction with US 17/GA 25. GHM 015-12, 1959.)

FORT ARGYLE

Near here, on the West bank of the Ogeechee River, Fort Argyle was built in 1733, to command one of the main passes by which enemy Indians had recently invaded South Carolina, and to give protection to the settlers of Savannah from anticipated raids by Spaniards from Florida.

The fort was named in honor of John, Duke of Argyle, friend and patron of James Edward Oglethorpe, and was garrisoned by Captain McPherson with a detachment of Rangers.

(Located on GA 144, 4.2 miles west of junction with US 17/GA 25. GHM 015-9, 1958.)

FORT McALLISTER – 4.5 MI.

East 4.5 miles, on Great Ogeechee River, Fort McAllister was built 1861-62 to guard the "back door" to Savannah. During 1862-63, it repulsed 7 attacks by armored vessels, some mounting 15-inch guns. Dec. 13, 1864, its small garrison of 230 Georgians was overwhelmed by Hazen's Division, 15th Corps (U), which had marched via this road. Its fall opened the Ogeechee to Union vessels, which, loaded with supplies for Gen. Sherman's army, had been lying in Tybee Roads and Port Royal Sound. A wharf and depot were built at King's Bridge (on US 17) from which these supplies were distributed to the invading forces.

(Located on GA 144, 5.4 miles east of junction with US 17/GA 25. GHM 015-5A, 1957.)

KILPATRICK ON BRYAN NECK

On Dec. 12, 1864, the 3rd Cavalry Division (U), Brig. Gen. J. L. Kilpatrick, USA, covering the right rear of Gen. Sherman's army which was then closing in on Savannah, crossed the Great Ogeechee River near Fort Argyle and the Canoochee River near Bryan Court House (Clyde) on pontoon bridges laid by the 1st Missouri Engineers (U) and moved down Bryan Neck. That night, Kilpatrick made his headquarters at the plantation home of Lt. Col. Joseph L. McAllister, 7th Georgia Cavalry (C), which stood near the river immediately north of this site.

On the 13th, Kilpatrick sent Murray's brigade into Liberty County to scout the country to Sunbury. He ordered Atkins' brigade and the 10th Wisconsin Battery to camp at "Cross Roads" (Richmond Hill) then, with two of Atkins' regiments, he moved down Bryan Neck. Approaching Fort McAllister, he skirmished with the Confederate pickets, driving them back to the fort. After examining the approaches to the fort he moved on the Kilkenny Bluff (8 miles SE) where he was able to make contact with the USS "Fernandina" and forward dispatches to the flagship (U) reporting the arrival of Gen. Sherman's army at Savannah.

On the 14th, Kilpatrick moved with the balance of his command to Midway Church. After scouting the country and stripping it of livestock and provisions he returned to Bryan County and went into camp at "Cross Roads" to picket the country to the south and west, and to protect the Union supply depot at King's Bridge.

(Located on GA 144, 5.4 miles east of junction with US 17/GA 25. GHM 015-13, 1959.)

HARDWICKE

This site on the Great Ogeechee, 14 miles from the Atlantic, was selected in 1755 by Governor John Reynolds for the capital of Georgia. He named it for his kinsman, Lord High Chancellor of England, Philip Yorke Hardwicke. Reynolds said: "Hardwicke has a charming situation, the winding of the river making it a peninsula and it is the only fit place for the capital." In 1761, Sir James Wright, the Province Governor, determined against the removal of the capital from Savannah. Hardwicke then became little more than a trading village and it is now listed among "the dead towns of Georgia."

(Located on GA 144 Spur. From US 17/GA 25 travel GA 144 East 5.4 miles, turn left onto GA 144 Spur and travel 2.1 miles to marker. DAC 015-95, 1968.)

FORT McALLISTER
THE NAVAL BOMBARDMENTS

On July 1st and 29th, 1862, the fort was shelled by Union gunboats and on Nov. 19th by the ironclad "Wissahickon" and two escort craft. Hit below the waterline, "Wissahickon" withdrew after firing 17 11-inch and 25 other shells. The escorts withdrew later after firing 49 100-pdr. and 42 other shells.

On Jan. 27, 1863, the armored monitor "Montauk," Comdr. J. L. Worden, USN, anchored near the fort, leaving her escort of four gunboats one mile astern. She fired 61 15-inch and 35 11-inch shells, the first use of

15-inch shells against a land battery. On Feb. 1st, "Montauk" and her escort shelled for five hours, killing Major John B. Gallie, CSA, wounding 7 gunners, and disabling 1 gun. On Feb. 28th, while her escort shelled the fort, "Montauk" destroyed the CSS "Nashville," aground 1400 yards NNW.

On Mar. 3rd, the monitors "Passaic," "Patapsco," and "Nahant," Capt. P. Drayton, USN, engaged the fort for eight hours with no more damage to either side than had been suffered in previous engagements. No further naval bombardments were attempted.

By act of the Confederate Congress, approved May 1, 1863, the defenders were thanked for their "gallantry and endurance."

(Located at Fort McAllister. From US 17/GA 25 travel GA 144 East 5.4 miles, turn left onto GA 144 Spur and travel 4.1 miles to marker. GHM 015-4, 1957.)

SINKING OF THE CSS "NASHVILLE (RATTLESNAKE)"

In July, 1862, the CSS "Nashville," Capt. Baker, ran the Union blockade and entered Savannah via Wilmington River with a cargo of arms. Loaded with cotton for Europe, she attempted to escape via Ossabaw Sound. Thwarted by the vigilance of the blockading squadron, she was withdrawn up Great Ogeechee River and refitted as a raider. Renamed "Rattlesnake," her silhouette was lowered and she received heavier guns. In February, 1863, ready for

OFFICIAL RECORDS NAVY

THE NASHVILLE, NOW REMAMED RATTLESNAKE, AS SHE APPEARED A SHORT TIME BEFORE HER DESTRUCTION

sea, she dropped down-river to Fort McAllister to plan her escape. On the 27th, she was forced to retire upstream upon the approach of the armored monitor "Montauk," Comdr. J. L. Worden, USN, and ran aground in Seven Mile Reach a short distance above the fort.

Early on the 28th, "Montauk" anchored near the fort and within 1200 yards of "Nashville (Rattlesnake)." She opened fire with 11 and 15-inch guns while her escort shelled the fort. Fires broke out and shortly "Nashville" was aflame fore and aft. At 9:20 her pivot gun burst, at 9:40 her funnel went by the board, and at 9:55 her magazine exploded, shattering her into smoking ruins. Although undamaged by direct hits from the fort's guns, "Montauk" struck a torpedo while dropping down-river which blew a hole in her bottom. She was beached in the mud for repairs.

(Located at Fort McAllister. From US 17/GA 25 travel GA 144 East 5.4 miles, turn left onto GA 144 Spur and travel 4.1 miles to marker. GHM 015-7, 1957.)

Sketched by Theodore R. Davis – Harper's Weekly, January 14, 1865

General Hazen's Division, Fifteenth Corps, Storming Fort McAllister, December 13, 1864

FORT McALLISTER
THE ASSAULT FROM THE REAR

Dec. 1864. Fort McAllister, built 1861-62 to close the Great Ogeechee River to enemy ships, mounted 11 seige guns, 12 field pieces and 1 10-inch mortar. Below it, piles and torpedoes obstructed the channel. As the Union forces neared Savannah, the fort's capture became imperative in order that ships could pass up-river to supply them. Naval attempts having failed, Brig. Gen. Wm. B. Hazen's Division,15th Corps (U), was ordered to cross the river, move to the fort, and take it from the rear.

At dawn on the 13th, Hazen crossed at King's Bridge, marched via "Cross Roads" (Richmond Hill) and Bryan Neck road (Ga 63), arriving about noon. At 4:45, after a difficult deployment, he assaulted the fort; by 5:00, his three brigades had swarmed over the works and overpowered individually Major Geo. W. Anderson's small garrison of 230 Georgians who fought gallantly to the end.

Gen. Sherman watched the assault from Dr. Cheves' rice mill, 2¹/₂ miles NNW across the river, after which he opened communications with Adm. Dahlgren's fleet (U), waiting in Ossabaw Sound.

Losses: (U) 24 killed, 110 wounded, total 134; (C) 14 killed, 21 wounded, 195 captured, total 230.

(Located at Fort McAllister. From US 17/GA 25 travel GA 144 East 5.4 miles, turn left onto GA 144 Spur and travel 4.1 miles to marker. GHM 015-03, 1958.)

CAMDEN COUNTY

Named in honor of Sir Charles Pratt, Earl of Camden (1714-1794), English jurist who opposed the English Ministry's attitude towards the colonies. County Seat: Woodbine.

KINGSLAND

ATLANTIC COASTAL HIGHWAY THROUGH GEORGIA

From South Carolina line to Florida line distance of 136 miles. Traversing Chatham, Bryan, Liberty, McIntosh, Glynn and Camden Counties. First work done in 1735 when the road from Savannah to Darien, probably the first road in Georgia, was laid out with the assistance of Tomochichi the Mico of the Yamacraws. Savannah River Bridge completed August 1925. Paving through Chatham County completed 1921. Construction from Chatham – Bryan County line to Florida line financed with State and Federal funds and a $900,000 bond issue of the Coastal Highway District. Construction program of the Coastal Highway District under the leadership of Harvey Granger, chairman of the Coastal Highway Commission. Begun August 1924 and completed October 1927.

Coastal Highway Commission

Harvey Granger, Chairman
Frank C. Battey, Sec. & Treas.
David S. Atkinson, Attorney
E. L. Stephens, Field Supt.
Porter G. Pierpont, Commissioner
Carl Mendel, Commisioner
Julius Morgan, Commissioner
A. F. Winn, Commissioner
R. M. Martin, Commissioner
W. E. Williams, Commissioner
Alfred Townsend, Commissioner
R. L. Phillips, Commissioner
A. K. Swift, Commissioner

State Highway Department

John N. Holder, Chairman of the Board
Stanley S. Bennet, Member of the Board
John R. Phillips, Member of the Board
W. R. Neel, State Highway Engineer
Searcy B. Slack, Bridge Engineer
H. J. Friedman, Division Engineer

(Located on US 17 at the Georgia
/Florida State line. ACH 020-99,
1930.) ♦ ★ – not standing.

ROAD TO COLRAINE – 1796

Monument there commemorating
treaty of friendship, 1796, between
Creek Indians and the United
States, signed by Benjamin Hawkins
and others.

(Located on US 17 at junction with
GA 40. ACH 020-98, 1930.) ♦ ★
– not standing.

ST. MARYS

CITY OF ST. MARYS

This town was built on the north
bank of the St. Marys River at a
place called Buttermilk Bluff. Origi-
nal tract of land containing 1620
acres was purchased by the propri-
etors for laying out the Town of St.
Marys from Jacob Weed for thirty-
eight dollars on Dec. 12, 1787. City
first laid out by James Finley, County
Surveyor, Aug. 1788 and recorded
Jan. 5, 1789. The twenty proprietors
of the town were: Isaac Wheeler,
William Norris, Nathaniel Ashley,
William Ashley, Lodowick Ashley,
James Seagrove, James Finley, John
Fleming, Robert Seagrove, Henry
Osborne, Thomas Norris, Jacob
Weed, John Alexander, Langley
Bryant, Jonathan Bartlett, Stephen
Conyers, William Ready, Prentis
Gallup, Simeon Dillingham, Richard
Cole.

City laid out second time as authorized by an Act of Dec. 5, 1792. Map
of town drawn by Parker, Hopkins,
& Meers, certified by James Parker,
County Surveyor, Jan. 3, 1792.
Town of St. Marys was incorporated
by an Act passed Nov. 26, 1802.

St. Marys temporary county seat
until first courthouse and Gaol
erected at Jefferson (Jeffersonton) as
authorized and named in Act passed
Nov. 29, 1800. Jeffersonton was permanent county seat for sixty-nine
years (1801-1871).

Election held Jan. 3, 1871 authorized
by Act passed Oct. 27, 1870 for
removal of county seat from Jeffer-

sonton to St. Marys. St. Marys permanent county seat for fifty-two years (1871-1923). Act of Aug. 11, 1923 authorized removal of county seat from St. Marys to Woodbine.

(Located at Osborne and Dillingham Streets. GHM 020-10, 1954.)

FIRST PRESBYTERIAN CHURCH

Built by public subscription in 1808 as a place of divine worship for the inhabitants of St. Marys and its vicinity. Reverend Horace Southworth Pratt was ordained and installed as the first pastor by the Presbytery of Georgia in June, 1822.

Incorporated under the name of the Independent Presbyterian Church of St. Marys Dec. 20, 1828. On Dec. 5, 1832, was incorporated as the First Presbyterian Church of St. Marys in the Georgia Presbytery.

(Located at Osborne and Conyers Streets. GHM 020-1, 1953.)

WASHINGTON PUMP & OAK

There were originally six wells one in each square, the only source of pure water for St. Marys, (until the tidal wave of 1818).

On the day that the Father of His Country was buried at Mt. Vernon local services were also held throughout the nation. St. Marys citizens marched to the dock to meet a boat bearing a flag draped casket; bore it up Osborn St., and with due ceremony and firing of guns, buried it where the Well known as the "Washington Pump" now is.

To mark the spot, four oaks were planted and have since been known as the "Washington Oaks." Only this one remains. This well was driven the year of Washington's burial and has ever since been called the "Washington Pump."

(Located at Osborne and Conyers Streets. GHM 020-3, 1953.) **Note:** The last Washington Oak is no longer standing.

COURTESY, GEORGIA DEPARTMENT OF ARCHIVES AND HISTORY

WASHINGTON PUMP & OAK

ST. MARYS
METHODIST CHURCH
ESTABLISHED 1799-1800
CELEBRATED SESQUI-CENTENNIAL 1949

This church is the oldest religious organization in the city, although not the oldest church building. George Clark served as first missionary to the people here in 1792. John Garvin was the first appointed Pastor to St. Marys in 1799. Methodist services were first held in the building erected for a Courthouse.

In 1812 the City of St. Marys deeded Methodists a lot 200 x 200 ft., still in use at this time. Church built after 1812 was in use until a few years before the Civil War when the old church was moved to another site and given to the Negro Methodists. Present church was built before the Civil War. While St. Marys was occupied by Federal troops in 1862, this church was used as a Quartermaster's Dept. where animals were butchered.

A deed was granted the church in 1878. The building was renovated on several occasions. Between 1792-1955, 103 Pastors have served this church. It was the first charge of Bishop Arthur J. Moore in 1909.

(Located on Conyers Street just east of Osborne Street. GHM 020-11, 1955.)

FIRST PECAN TREES
GROWN HERE ABOUT 1840

Grown from pecan nuts found floating at sea by Capt. Samuel F. Flood

and planted by his wife, nee Rebecca Grovenstine, on Block 47.

The remainder of these nuts were planted by St. Joseph Sebastian Arnow in the north half of Block 26.

These first plantings produced large and heavy-bearing trees, as did their nuts and shoots in turn. Taken from St. Marys to distant points throughout southeastern states they became famous before the Texas pecan was generally known.

(Located in the 200 block of Weed Street near junction with Ready Street. GHM 020-4, 1953.)

POINT PETER

East of here, at the junction of Peter Creek and St. Mary's river, the British built Fort Tonyn in 1776; controlling the southern part of the colony of Georgia for two years.

In 1778, American Revolutionary forces, both land and water, forced evacuation of the exposed position. The English retreated N. W. along North river into Pagan Creek Plantation, home of the Tories, Charles and Jermyn Wright, brothers of Royal Governor James Wright.

On high land along Alligator (now Borell) creek, they built log and sand breastworks and repulsed the American Cavalry under Col. Elijah Clark.

It appears that in the war of 1812, Fort Pickering was built on the Fort Tonyn site.

(Located at Osborne Street and Point Peter Road. GHM 020-8B, 1953.)

TABBY SUGAR WORKS OF JOHN HOUSTOUN McINTOSH

These are the ruins of a tabby sugar works built by John Houstoun McIntosh at New Canaan Plantation soon after 1825. In his sugar house McIntosh installed what was, according to Thomas Spalding, the first horizontal cane mill worked by cattle power.

McIntosh, born in 1773 in what is now McIntosh County, settled in East Florida as a young man and became the leader of a group of American citizens who, during the War of 1812, plotted the annexation of East Florida to the United States. This plot crushed by the Spanish government, McIntosh removed to Georgia and acquired two planta-tions in Camden County, Marianna, where he built a home, and New Canaan, where he began the cultiva-tion of sugar cane under the influ-ence of Thomas Spalding, who had experimented in sugar production and seen the use of steam-propelled horizontal cane mills in Louisiana.

After McIntosh's death in 1836, New Canaan was sold to one Col. Hallowes, who changed the name of the plantation to Bollingbrook and lived there until after the Civil War. During the war, Hallowes planted cane and made sugar in the McIn-tosh sugar house. He also used the tabby sugar works as a starch factory, producing arrowroot starch in large quantities.

(Located on GA 40 Spur, 2.9 miles south of junction with GA 40, in park near the entrance to Kings Bay Submarine Base. GHM 020-12, 1963.)

this page and previous page
RUINS OF THE TABBY SUGAR WORKS
BUILT BY JOHN HOUSTOUN MCINTOSH, C.1825

WOODBINE

CAMDEN COUNTY

Formed from old Colonial parishes: St. Mary and St. Thomas. Camden one of eight original counties of Georgia created by the State Constitution of 1777. County named for Charles Pratt, Earl of Camden, Chief Justice and Lord Chancellor of England. Camden County gave territory to Wayne in 1808 and 1812, and to Charlton in 1854. St. Marys was temporary County Site until Jefferson (Jeffersonton) was named as first permanent county site by an Act of Nov. 29, 1800. Jefferson seat of government sixty-nine years (1801-1871). Election held Jan. 3, 1871, authorized county seat be removed from Jefferson to St. Marys. St. Marys county seat for fifty-two years (1871-1923). Act of Aug. 11, 1923 authorized removal of county seat from St. Marys to Woodbine. Present courthouse here erected 1928.

Some of first and early settlers of the county were: Talmage Hall, James Woodland, Thomas Stafford, David & Hugh Brown, John King, John Hardee, Henry Osborne, Jacob Weed, John Webb, Abner Williams, Charles & John Floyd, Nathan Atkinson, Isaac & Richard Lang, Joseph Hull, William Berrie, Thomas Miller, John Bailey, Sr., and nephew, John Bailey and Lewis DuFour.

First County officers were: Alexander Semple, Clerk of Court; Wilson Williams, Sheriff; John Crawford, Coroner; Nathaniel Ashley,Tax Col. Robert Brown, Register of Probates.

A number of the early settlers of this county came from Acadia, San Domingo, Minorca, and Spanish East Florida.

(Located on US 17 at 4th Street. GHM 020-9, 1954.) **Note:** Courthouse is two blocks east on 4th Street.

REFUGE PLANTATION

On the Satilla River 2.8 miles from here, was one of the largest rice plantations in the South. Originally a crown grant of 500 acres to George McIntosh in 1765, it passed to his son, John Houston McIntosh. In 1836 Gen. Duncan Lamont Clinch, U.S. Army hero of the Seminole War and husband of Eliza Bayard McIntosh, daughter of John Houston McIntosh, settled here. He farmed until 1844, then entered politics. Elected to Congress on the Whig ticket in 1844, he served through 1845. Born in Edgecombe Co., N. C., Apr. 6, 1787, Gen. Clinch died Nov. 27, 1849 in Macon, Ga. His plantation remained in the family until 1905.

(Located on US 17/GA 25, 1.2 miles north. GHM 020-6, 1986.)

FLOYDS' FAIRFIELD AND BELLVIEW PLANTATIONS

Charles Floyd and son John moved to Camden Co. and established rice plantations on the Satilla river about 1800.

John Floyd (1769-1839) was a noted general and hero in War of 1812; a

BELLVIEW PLANTATION HOUSE RUINS

state legislator, U.S. Congressman and presidential elector.

Outer walls of Bellview plantation home were built in shape of anchor, and still stand.

Charles Rinaldo Floyd, son of General John Floyd, filled many military positions of high trust. Was a Georgia legislator and talented artist.

Burial ground for members of family is on plantations. Handsome U.S. Monuments mark the graves of Charles, John and Charles Rinaldo.

(Located on US 17/GA 25, 2.4 miles south at Colesburg. GHM 020-2, 1953.)

POST ROAD

This road, formerly an Indian trail which parallelled the coast, was used by the Spanish and the British. In 1778 it was travelled by Revolutionary soldiers who marched against Fort Tonyn at Point Peter. Albert Gallatin while U.S. Secretary of the Treasury in 1805 recommended the Old St. Marys Road, a portion of the Post Road, as one of seven principal routes that were important to U.S. defense and postal service.

(Located on US 17/GA 25, 7.4 miles south at Kinlaw Road or 4.4 miles north of Kingsland. GHM 020-5, 1953.)

BURNT FORT

"Public Works" including a block-house erected at Burnt Fort Station on Satilla River opposite old town of New Hanover which became known as Burnt Fort.

Built by order of Capt. John F. Randolph of Camden County in 1793 for the protection of the county against raids of Creek Indians.

In 1794 a troop of Military Dragoons of Camden County was stationed here under the command of Capt. John F. Randolph in the service of the United States.

(Located on GA 252 at Burnt Fort Station. GHM 020-7, 1953.) ♦ ★ – not standing.

CHATHAM COUNTY

Named in honor of William Lord Pitt, the Earl of Chatham (1708-1778), noted prime minister of England, who vigorously opposed the harsh measures taken with regard to the American colonies in 1774-75. Chatham was an original county, previously organized in 1758 as the parishes of Saint Philip and Christ Church. County Seat: Savannah.

POOLER

SHERMAN AT POOLER

On Dec. 9, 1864, troops of Mower's division, 17th Corps, of Gen. Sherman's army (U), which was closing in on Savannah, advanced to Pooler after suffering losses through the day from artillery mounted on a RR flat car, torpedoes planted on the roads, and the stubborn resistance of Confederate infantry. By evening, Pooler had been seized and a strong line had been established astride the RR, on the road passing by the depot. An advance line was constructed about 300 yards farther east.

That night, Gen. Sherman and Gen. Blair (17th Corps) established headquarters in Pooler, about 300 yards west of the depot, the former on the north side of the road.

(Located on US 80 at the First Baptist Church. GHM 025-70, 1958.)

PORT WENTWORTH

INDIAN TRADING POST: HOME OF MARY MUSGROVE

During the first years after the founding of the Colony of Georgia in 1733 these lands (now owned by the Savannah Sugar Refining Company) were known as the "Grange" or "Cowpen" plantation. Along the Savannah River, about one mile East of this marker, was located the home of John Musgrove and his wife, Mary, who engaged there in the Indian trade and in farming and cattle raising.

Mary Musgrove, famed in Georgia history for her services to James Edward Oglethorpe as interpreter, was a half-breed whose Indian name was "Cousaponakeesa." She was a niece of Old Brim, Emperor of the Creek Indians. The Musgrove house was a seat of hospitality. Among the important visitors entertained here was the celebrated John Wesley.

During the nineteenth century these lands were known as Colerain Plantation. They were extensively cultivated. Colerain was one of the largest rice plantations on the Savannah River. In Ante-Bellum days near the former site of the Musgrove house stood one of the finest mansions on the River, the home of James Potter, owner of Colerain.

The erection in 1916 of the Savannah Sugar Refining Company plant on this property marked the beginning of the transition from Savannah's cotton and naval stores economy to that of a leading industrial seaport.

(Located on US 17/GA 25 at the Savannah Sugar Refining Co. GHM 025-78, 1961.) **Note:** A duplicate marker is located at the end of the entrance drive next to the guard house.

BATTLE BETWEEN CONFEDERATE GUNBOATS AND UNION FIELD ARTILLERY
(DECEMBER 12, 1864)

In December, 1864, was fought on the Savannah River near here one of the few battles in which Confederate gunboats and Union field artillery were engaged against each other.

Colerain Plantation, as these lands were then known, had been occupied on December 10, 1864, by units of Sherman's army. Anticipating an attempt by a Confederate naval flotilla, which had been engaged in protecting a railroad bridge further upstream, to return to Savannah, Captain C. E. Winegar's battery was posted on a bluff about one mile East of this marker.

Early on the morning of December 12, 1864, the CSS *Sampson* and *Macon* and their tender, the *Resolute*, attempted to run past the Federal battery. There was a "terrific fire" from both sides, according to John Thomas Scharf, a midshipman on the *Sampson* who later became the well-known historian of the Confederate States Navy. The gunboats were struck several times.

Unable to get past the battery, the vessels turned about. In doing so the *Resolute* collided with the gunboats and drifted helplessly upon Argyle Island where she was captured by troops of the 3rd Wisconsin Regiment. With the aid of barrels of bacon thrown in their furnaces, the two gunboats were able to steam out of range. They escaped to Augusta.

(Located on US 17/GA 25 at the Savannah Sugar Refining Co. GHM 025-79, 1961.) **Note:** A duplicate marker is located at the end of the entrance drive next to the guard house.

MULBERRY GROVE PLANTATION

Mulberry Grove which is located approximately 3 miles northwest from this marker is one of the most historic of the old Savannah River plantations.

In early Colonial days mulberry trees were cultivated at Mulberry Grove for use in Georgia's silk industry. Later it became one of the leading rice plantations of Georgia. At the end of the Revolution the plantation, which had belonged to Lieutenant Governor John Graham, a Royalist, was granted by the State of Georgia to Major General Nathanael Greene as a reward for his military services. General Greene was residing at Mulberry Grove at the time of his death on June 12, 1786.

In 1793 Eli Whitney, who was the tutor of the Greene children, invented the cotton gin at Mulberry Grove. The following year a large ginning machine was erected at the plantation. Its foundation still stands there.

(Located on US 17/GA 25 at City Hall. GHM 025-39, 1956.)

MULBERRY GROVE

Colonial Plantation of John Graham, Lieutenant-Governor of Province of Georgia. Granted 1783, by State of Georgia to General Nathaniel Greene, who died here 1786.

Here Eli Whitney invented the Cotton Gin, 1793.

(Located on US 17/GA 25 at City Hall. DAR 025-173, 1936.)

ROAD TO MULBERRY GROVE PLANTATION

Where Eli Whitney invented cotton gin. Once owned by the Royal Lieutenant Governor Graham. Later presented by State of Georgia to General Nathanael Greene, who died here June 19, 1786.

(Located on US 17/GA 25 near City Hall. ACH 025-172, 1930.) ♦ ★ – not standing.

ATLANTIC COASTAL HIGHWAY THROUGH GEORGIA

From South Carolina line to Florida line distance of 136 miles. Traversing Chatham, Bryan, Liberty, McIntosh, Glynn and Camden Counties. First work done in 1735 when the road from Savannah to Darien, probably the first road in Georgia, was laid out with the assistance of Tomochichi the Mico of the Yamacraws. Savannah River Bridge completed August 1925. Paving through Chatham County completed 1921. Construction from Chatham – Bryan County line to Florida line financed with State and Federal funds and a $900,000 bond issue of the Coastal Highway District. Construction program of the Coastal Highway District under the leadership of Harvey Granger, chairman of the Coastal Highway Commission. Begun August 1924 and completed October 1927.

Coastal Highway Commission

Harvey Granger, Chairman
Frank C. Battey, Sec. & Treas.
David S. Atkinson, Attorney
E. L. Stephens, Field Supt.
Porter G. Pierpont, Commissioner
Carl Mendel, Commissioner
Julius Morgan, Commissioner
A. F. Winn, Commissioner
R. M. Martin, Commissioner
W. E. Williams, Commissioner
Alfred Townsend, Commissioner
R. L. Phillips, Commissioner
A. K. Swift, Commissioner

State Highway Department

John N. Holder, Chairman of the Board
Stanley S. Bennet, Member of the Board
John R. Phillips, Member of the Board
W. R. Neel, State Highway Engineer
Searcy B. Slack, Bridge Engineer
H. J. Friedman, Division Engineer

(Located on US 17/GA 25 at the Georgia/South Carolina State line. ACH 020-171, 1930.)

BLUE STAR MEMORIAL HIGHWAY

A tribute to the Armed Forces
that have defended
the United States of America.

(Located on I-95 at the Georgia Welcome Center. GCG 025-170.)

SAVANNAH

WILLIAM BARTRAM TRAIL
TRACED 1773-1777

In 1765 John and William Bartram, naturalists, began an extended trail from Savannah through Georgia and left a legacy of impressions.

Erected by The Oleander District of the Garden Club of Georgia, Inc. in cooperation with the Garden Club of Georgia, Inc., The City of Savannah, Georgia.

(Located at River and Barnard Streets. GCG 025-181, 1985.)

JOHN RYAN'S EXCELSIOR BOTTLE WORKS

On this site in 1852 stood the Excelsior Bottle Works operated by John Ryan for the manufacture of soda water and other carbonated beverages. Ryan's soda, in colorful bottles embossed with his name and location, was known throughout Georgia. His operations expanded to Augusta, Columbus and Atlanta. Today Ryan's bottles are prized by collectors nationwide.

John Ryan, with his contemporaries, Thomas Maher and James Ray, is commemorated for his pioneer contribution to the soda water industry in Georgia and the United States. Ryan retired from business in 1879 and passed away in Savannah on March 23, 1885.

(Located at Bay and Montgomery Streets. GHM/GHR 025-169, 1976.)

EVACUATION OF SAVANNAH

On Dec. 14, 1864, Fort McAllister (C) having fallen the day before, opening the Great Ogeechee River to Union shipping and rendering Savannah untenable, Lt. Gen. W. J. Hardee, CSA, decided to evacuate the city to save it from a destructive bombardment and to extricate his besieged army. River craft being unequal to the task, and no pontoon bridging being available, an engineering expedient was adopted. Directed by Lt. Col. B. W. Frobel, CSA, pontoon type bridges were laid by sailors of the CS Navy and details from the Georgia Militia. Using large "cotton flats" for boats, car wheels for anchors and planks from the city wharves for flooring, a bridge was laid from the foot of West Broad Street to Hutchinson Island, another across Back River to Pennyworth Island, and a third across Little Back River to the South Carolina shore.

On the 19th, orders were issued giving priorities and times of withdrawal. The heavy guns were spiked and carriages and ammunition destroyed. At dark, the garrisons of Whitemarsh Island were withdrawn into the city and evacuated via the bridges.

At dark, on the 20th, the garrisons of Causton's Bluff, Thunderbolt and the Savannah River batteries gathered at Fort Jackson and were transferred by steamer to Screven's Ferry; but the main garrison – infantry, cavalry, light artillery and wagons – crossed on the bridges. Well before dawn, the rear-guard had cleared Hutchinson Island, the bridge from

West Broad Street had been cut adrift, and the troops were marching via the Union Causeway to Hardeeville.

(Located at Bay and Jefferson Streets, in the park. GHM 025-52, 1957.)

OGLETHORPE'S BENCH

OGLETHORPE'S CAMPING GROUND
(GEORGIA'S FOUNDING)

February 12, 1733, Oglethorpe with 125 colonists, landed. That night pitched his tent beneath three pines on this bluff. Granite memorial seat marks spot.

(Located at Bull and Bay Streets, next to City Hall. ACH 025-199, 1930.) ♦ ★ – not standing.

LANDING OF OGLETHORPE AND THE COLONISTS

James Edward Oglethorpe, the founder of Georgia, landed with the original colonists, about 114 in number, at the foot of this bluff on February 1 (February 12, new style), 1733. The site where he pitched his tent is marked by the stone bench located about 100 feet west of this marker.

GENERAL JAMES EDWARD OGLETHORPE (1696-1785)

Savannah was for more than 100 years built according to Oglethorpe's unique city plan. Bull Street, the principal street of the city, is named in honor of Colonel William Bull of Charleston, S.C., who assisted Oglethorpe in laying out the city.

The colonists sailed in the ship *Anne* from Gravesend, England, November 17, 1732; landed at Charles Town, S.C., January 13, 1733; proceeded later to Beaufort, S.C., and thence, in small boats, through the inland waterway to Yamacraw Bluff. The town site had already been selected by Oglethorpe in friendly negotiation with Tomo-chi-chi, Mico of the Yamacraws, and with Mary Musgrove, the English-speaking, half-breed Indian princess who later, as niece of Emperor Brim of the Creek Nation, claimed sovereignty of southeastern Georgia.

(Located at Bull and Bay Streets, next to City Hall. GHM 025-1, 1982.)

UNITED STATES CUSTOMHOUSE

The U.S. Customhouse stands on historic ground. In a house on this site James Edward Oglethorpe, founder of the colony of Georgia, lived for a time, and in 1736 John Wesley preached his first sermon at Savannah in a building which stood on the rear of the lot.

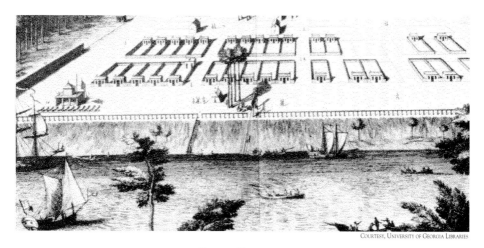

PLAN OF SAVANNAH
PREPARED IN 1734 FOR THE TRUSTEES "BY THEIR HONOURS OBLIGED AND MOST OBEDIENT SERVANT, PETER GORDON."

STAIRWAY OF THE CUSTOMHOUSE

The cornerstone of the Customhouse was laid in 1848. The building was completed in 1852 at a cost of $146,000. Built of granite from Quincy, Mass., the structure is one of the most handsome and substantial public buildings erected in that era. The magnificent fluted columns have tobacco leaves as capitals instead of the traditional decorations. The columns, each weighing fifteen tons, were brought to Savannah by sailing vessels. The unusual inside stairway divides at one-half height forming into circular stairs with no perpendicular support.

Although the building is used primarily by the United States Customs Service, it houses several Federal agencies. In earlier years it also served as a Post Office and Federal courthouse. In 1859-1860 the celebrated cases growing out of slave-running by the yacht "Wanderer" were tried here before Justice Wayne of the U. S. Supreme Court.

(Located at Bull and Bay Streets. GHM 025-57, 1957.)

SS SAVANNAH AND SS JOHN RANDOLPH

The first steamship to cross the Atlantic Ocean, the SS SAVANNAH, sailed from this harbor on May 22, 1819 and reached Liverpool 27 days later. The anniversary of her sailing, May 22, is celebrated as National Maritime Day. Captain

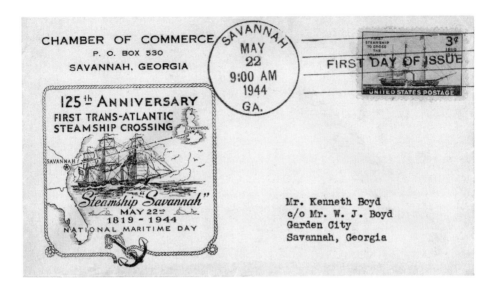

Moses Rogers was her master. James Monroe, President of the United States, inspected the vessel here and was taken on a trial excursion on May 12. The Savannah Steamship Company (of which William Scarbrough was principal promoter), fitted her with a 90 H.P. engine and boiler. She was of 350 tons burden, 98'6" long, 25'2" breadth, 12'11" draft, equipped with paddle-wheels, spars, and sails. She depended primarily upon sail power in the open seas. Before returning to Savannah she visited St. Petersburg, Crondstadt, and Stockholm.

The SS JOHN RANDOLPH, America's first successful iron steamship in commerce, was launched in this harbor July 9, 1834. Prefabricated in Birkenhead, England, for Gazaway B. Lamar of Savannah, she was shipped in segments and assembled here. She was 100' long and 22' breadth. Unlike the SS SAVANNAH, she was an immediate commercial success in the river trade, and was the first of a great fleet of iron steamboats on the rivers of America.

(Located at Bull and Bay Streets next to City Hall. GHM 025-3, 1952.)

CHATHAM ARTILLERY'S "WASHINGTON GUNS"

These bronze cannon were presented to the Chatham Artillery by President Washington after his visit to Savannah in 1791. Of English and French make, respectively, they are excellent examples of the art of ordnance manufacture in the 18th century.

An inscription on the British 6 pounder states that it was "surrendered by the capitulation of York Town Oct. 19, 1781." The English cannon was cast in 1758 during the reign of George II and the royal insignia and motto of the Order of the Garter appear on its barrel.

The French gun was manufactured at Strasburg in 1756. On its elaborately engraved barrel appear the coat of arms of Louis XIV; the sun which was the emblem of that monarch, and a Latin inscription (which Louis XIV first ordered placed on French cannon) meaning "Last Argument of Kings." The dolphins were emblematic of the Dauphin of France. The gun was individually named "La Populaire."

Reminders of America's hard-won struggle for Independence and of the great man who led the Continental forces in the Revolution, the historic "Washington Guns" were placed on public display here through the co-operation of the Chatham Artillery and the City of Savannah.

(Located at Bay and Drayton Streets in the park near the Old Savannah Cotton Exchange. GHM 025-53, 1982.)

CARROLL PROCTOR SCRUGGS

ONE OF THE CHATHAM ARTILLERY'S
"WASHINGTON GUNS"

CHATHAM ARTILLERY'S "WASHINGTON GUNS"

These cannon, which were captured when Lord Cornwallis surrendered at Yorktown in the American Revolution, were a gift to the Chatham Artillery by President George Washington – a mark of his appreciation for the part the local military company played in the celebration of his visit to Savannah in May, 1791. Washington commended the Chatham Artillery in "warmest terms" and at one of the functions in his honor (which took place on the river bluff east of this spot) proposed a toast "to the present dexterous Corps of Artillery."

The "Washington Guns" have thundered a welcome to many distinguished visitors to Savannah, including James Monroe, the Marquis de Lafayette, James K. Polk, Millard Fillmore, Chester A. Arthur, Jefferson Davis, Grover Cleveland, William McKinley, William H. Taft, and Franklin D. Roosevelt.

During the War Between the States the historic cannon were buried for safety beneath the Chatham Artillery armory and were not removed until 1872 when the Federal occupation troops had departed.

The "Washington Guns" were taken to Yorktown in 1881 by a contingent of the Chatham Artillery and led the parade at the centennial celebration of Cornwallis' surrender.

(Located at Bay and Drayton Streets in the park near the Old Savannah Cotton Exchange. GHM 025-54, 1982.)

BIRTHPLACE OF THE UNIVERSITY OF GEORGIA
MEETING PLACE OF LEGISLATURE IN 1785

Directly across Bay Street from this marker formerly stood the brick building, built in late Colonial days and known as the "Coffee House," in which the Legislature of Georgia met in 1785. Owned by Thomas Stone, it was described in a newspaper advertisement in 1785 as having "ten large, cool, elegant rooms" and as "not equaled by any other house in the state" for "business, and conveniency for a large family."

While meeting in the house owned by Thomas Stone the House of Assembly of Georgia enacted on January 28, 1785, an act for the "establishment of a public seat of learning in this state" – the preamble reciting that it was "among the first objects of those who wish well to the national prosperity, to encourage and support the principals of religion and morality, and early to place the youth under the forming hand of society, that by instruction they may be moulded to the love of virtue and good order."

The charter granted to the Board of Trustees of the University of Georgia in 1785 was the first charter issued in the United States to a state university.

(Located at Bay and Drayton Streets in the park near the Old Savannah Cotton Exchange. GHM 025-46, 1957.)

OLD SAVANNAH COTTON EXCHANGE

The Savannah Cotton Exchange building was completed in 1887 during the era when Savannah ranked first as a cotton seaport on the Atlantic and second in the world. In its heyday as a cotton port over two million bales a year moved through Savannah. The Cotton Exchange was the center of activity in the staple which dominated this city's economic life before its evolution into a leading industrial seaport.

The Exchange was designed by the nationally-known Boston architect, William Gibbons Preston (1844-1910). His design won out in a competition participated in by eleven architects. The Exchange is believed to be one of the few structures in the world erected over an existing public street.

The beautiful iron railing around this grass plat, with panels featuring medallions of famous statesmen, authors and poets, once graced the ante-bellum Wetter House in Savannah.

The former Cotton Exchange is now the headquarters of the Savannah Chamber of Commerce, which cordially invites you to drop in for a visit.

(Located at Bay and Drayton Streets in the park near the Old Savannah

THE OLD SAVANNAH COTTON EXCHANGE

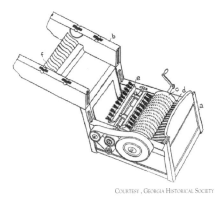

COURTESY, GEORGIA HISTORICAL SOCIETY

ORIGINAL MODEL OF WHITNEY'S COTTON GIN.

Cotton Exchange. GHM 025-56, 1957.) **Note:** The Chamber of Commerce no longer occupies this building.

THE INVENTION OF THE COTTON GIN
A HISTORICAL LANDMARK OF AGRICULTURAL ENGINEERING

This creative development which was responsible for the survival of the cotton industry in the United States occurred on General Nathaniel Greene's plantation near Savannah 10 miles northeast of this marker. Separation by hand labor of the lint from the seed of the desired upland variety of cotton produced only one pound per day per person.

Eli Whitney, a native of Massachusetts and Yale law graduate, came to Georgia to teach school in late 1792, at age 27. Mrs. Catherine Greene, widow of General Greene,

invited Whitney to her plantation, and urged him to design a cotton gin. He secluded himself for 10 days in the spring of 1793, with a basket of cotton bolls. He discovered that a hooked wire could pull the lint through a slot in the basket, leaving the seeds inside. In his patent application Whitney described the process as: consisting of spikes driven into a wooden cylinder and having a slotted bar through which these spikes passed and having a brush to clean the spikes, the result was a hand operated cotton gin which produced over 50 pounds per person per day. It was patented March 14, 1794.

Henry Ogden Holmes, of Georgia, a resourceful, practical mechanic on the Kincaide plantation of Fairfield County South Carolina, invented an improved gin and was granted a patent on May 12, 1796. His continuous flow gin used rip-saw teeth on a circular steel blade which passed through spaces between ribs. The circular saw gin with improvements, capable of giving 1000s of pounds per day, was still in use in 1985.

ELI WHITNEY (1765-1825)

Officials of the Cotton Exchange Commission building, which faces this marker, shipped from the port of Savannah thousands of bales to a new worldwide industry, and brought prosperity to the south.

(Located at Bay and Drayton Streets in the park near the Old Savannah Cotton Exchange. ASAE 025-198, 1986.)

SOLOMON'S LODGE NO. 1, F. & A. M.

Organized as a Masonic Lodge February 21, 1734, its first worshipful master was Gen. James Edward Oglethorpe, English soldier, statesman, humanitarian, and founder of Georgia, who raised the flag of England at Savannah on Feb. 12, 1733.

Chartered by the Grand Lodge of England in 1735 as "The Lodge at Savannah in ye province of Georgia." Solomon's is the oldest continuously operating English constituted Lodge in the Western Hemisphere. In 1786 the independent Grand Lodge of Georgia, F.&A.M. was created and proclaimed by concerted action of Solomon's and the one other Lodge then existing in the state. Solomon's was chartered the first Lodge of Georgia.

From its beginning in 1734 brethren of Solomon's Lodge have served with distinction in vital positions of leadership in public and fraternal affairs of city, colony, state and nation. The Lodge produced the first Grand Master of Georgia, F.&A.M., William Stephens who governed the Georgia craft from 1786-1788 and 1793-1813.

Solomon's Lodge, one of Savannah's greatest historical institutions is honored and revered by the nearly 100,00 freemasons of this state as the Mother Lodge of Georgia. Free and accepted Masons. Marker placed by the Educational Historical Commission Grand Lodge of Georgia, F.&A.M.

(Located at Bay and Drayton Streets in the park near the Old Savannah Cotton Exchange. GLG 025-197, 1969.)

OLD CITY EXCHANGE BELL

OLD CITY EXCHANGE BELL

This bell, which is believed to be the oldest in Georgia, bears the date 1802. Imported from Amsterdam, it hung in the cupola of the City Exchange from 1804 until a short time before that building was razed to make way for the present City Hall.

In its day, the bell signalled the closing time for shops and was rung by a watchman when fire broke out. Its rich tones were heard in celebration of American victories during the War of 1812. It pealed a welcome to such distinguished visitors to Savannah as Monroe, LaFayette, Polk, Fillmore, Clay and Webster and it tolled tributes for America's illustrious dead.

The tower of the City Exchange, where the bell hung, was a favorite resort of those anxious about the arrival of vessels. The replica of the tower in which the historic bell presently reposes was erected in 1957 through the combined efforts of the Savannah Chamber of Commerce, the Pilot Club of Savannah and the Savannah-Chatham Historic Site and Monument Commission.

(Located at Bay and Drayton Streets in the park near the Old Savannah Cotton Exchange. GHM 025-41, 1957.)

THE GEORGIA HUSSARS
ORGANIZED 13 FEBRUARY 1736

This Troop of Mounted Rangers was raised by Gen. Oglethorpe to patrol and protect the Colony of Georgia from the Spaniards and Indians. It fought at Bloody Marsh in 1742 and at the Siege of Savannah in 1779. Its record during the War 1861-65 is unsurpassed as was its service in Mexico, World War I, World War II and Korea. It remained Horse Cavalry until October 1940. From Colonial times to Vietnam, Hussars have represented Savannah in all our wars. It is still an active unit in the Georgia Army National Guard.

(Located at Bay and Lincoln Streets in the park. FWMC 025-196, 1968.)

SAVANNAH'S OLD HARBOR LIGHT
ERECTED IN 1858, IT STANDS 77 FEET ABOVE RIVER LEVEL.

OLD HARBOR LIGHT

This beacon light was erected by the federal government in 1858 as an aid to navigation of the Savannah River. Standing 77 feet above river level and illuminated by gas, it served for several years as a guide to vessels passing over the hulls of ships that the British scuttled in 1779 to close the harbor to the French naval forces. During the Siege of Savannah that year by the French and Americans the warship *Truite*, commanded by the Count de Chastenet de Puysegur, shelled this area of Savannah from her anchorage in Back River opposite this point.

The development of this portion of Emmet Park as a garden area was a project of the Trustees Garden Club during the centennial year of the erection of the "Old Harbor Light."

(Located at Bay and East Broad Streets in Emmet Park. GHM 025-68, 1958.)

THE TRUSTEES' GARDEN

At this site was located the first public agricultural experimental garden in America. From this garden was disseminated the upland cotton which later comprised the greater part of the world's cotton commerce Here were propagated and from this garden distributed, the peach trees which gave Georgia and South Carolina another major commercial crop.

The garden consisted of ten acres. It was established by Oglethorpe within one month after the settlement of Georgia. Botanists were sent by the Trustees of the Colony from England to the West Indies and South America to procure plants for the garden. Vine cuttings, flax, hemp, potashes, indigo, cochineal, olives, and medicinal herbs were grown. The greatest hope was centered in the mulberry trees, essential to silk culture. In the early days of the Colony, Queen Caroline was clothed in Georgia silk, and the town's largest structure was the filature.

The silk and wine industries failed to materialize. The distant sponsors were unable to judge of the immense importance of the experiments conducted in other products. In 1755 the site was developed as a residential section.

(Located off Bay and East Broad Streets in the Trustees' Garden parking lot next to the Pirates' House Restaurant. GHM 025-2, 1952.)

FORT WAYNE 1812

On old Trustees' Gardens of Colonial days, known as "The Fort" in Revolution when British captured city. Improved for War of 1812. Sold by United States to gas company 1850.

(Located off Bay and East Broad Streets in the Trustees' Garden parking lot next to the Pirates' House Restaurant. ACH 025-195, 1930.)
♦ ★ – not standing.

THE GEORGIA MEDICAL SOCIETY

The first Medical Society in Georgia, sixth oldest in America, was organized June 28, 1804, and continues to be active in Savannah today. Dr. Noble Wimberly Jones, first President, was the son of a member of General Oglethorpe's first settlers of 1733.

Dr. Samuel Roberio Nunez, first practicing physician, arrived July 10, 1733, with the second expedition to the new colony. He arrived in time to treat successfully a raging epidemic of dysentery.

In 1740, the first clinic for the poor opened at nearby Bethesda under Dr. John Hunter and Reverend George Whitefield, who previously had founded America's oldest orphanage there.

The Georgia Medical Society adopted the state's first Code of Medical Ethics, achieved a program of systematic vaccination against smallpox, carried out health surveys of Savannah and surrounding counties, founded a Medical Library, formed the first systematic anti-malarial effort begun in the United States, and conducted extensive studies of Savannah's major epidemic diseases – malaria, yellow fever, and smallpox.

(Located in Washington Square at Houston and St. Julian Streets. GMS 025-194, 1983.)

COURTESY, NATIONAL PORTRAIT GALLERY, LONDON

JOHN WESLEY (1703-1791)
A PORTRAIT (CIRCA 1766) BY NATHANIEL HONE

JOHN WESLEY, 1703-1791
FOUNDER OF METHODISM

On the "trust lot" south of President Street and immediately west of this square stood in 1736-37 the parsonage in which John Wesley resided. In the adjoining garden he read, prayed and meditated.

Weekly meetings of members of his Christ Church congregation were held in the small wooden dwelling. According to Wesley, "The first rise of Methodism was in 1729 when four of us met together at Oxford. The second was at Savannah in 1736 when twenty or thirty persons met at my house."

The monument here was dedicated in 1969. Wesley is depicted at the period of his Georgia ministry, wearing his Church of England vestments. The sculptor, Marshall Daugherty, says of this rendering:

"The moment is as he looks up from his Bible toward his congregation, about to speak and stretching out his right hand in love, invitation and exhortation. In contrast, the hand holding the Bible is intense and powerful – the point of contact with the Almighty…"

(Located in Reynolds Square at Abercorn and St. Julian Streets. GHM 025-88, 1969.)

JOHN WESLEY'S AMERICAN PARISH - SAVANNAH

Wesley, an Anglican minister, served as the religious leader of the Georgia colony from February 6, 1736 to December 1737. Seeking to minister to all, he led services in English, French, German, Spanish, and Italian.

Honor was accorded John Wesley, founder of Methodism, and this New World area where he lived and worked, by the declaration of the 1976 United Methodist General Conference that his "American Parish" be a United Methodist National Historic Landmark.

The landmark encompasses:
1. the Cockspur Island landing on US 80E
2. the site of Wesley's first sermon preached at Bay Lane and Bull Street
3. the Wesley monument (Reynolds Square)
4. the site of Wesley's parsonage and garden at Congress and Abercorn
5. the site of regular services at Wright Square and Bull Street

(Located in Reynolds Square at Abercorn and St. Julian Streets. UMC 025-193, 1976.)

ITALIANS IN GEORGIA'S GENESIS

When James Oglethorpe left England to begin the new colony of Georgia, in 1732, one of the passengers was Paul Amatis, an Italian artisan, skilled in producing silk. He was later placed in charge of Trustees Garden. Later, more Italian families came to pursue the task of producing silk. Joseph Ottolenghe is responsible for erecting a public filature in Savannah, on what is now Reynolds Square. It was at this filature that a one time record number of 15,212 pounds of cocoons was delivered for processing into raw silk. High hopes for success in this undertaking is exemplified on one side of the original Georgia Seal which depicts a mulberry leaf, a silkworm, and a cocoon with the encircled words: "Non sibi sed aliis": "Not for ourselves but for others."

(Located in Reynolds Square at Abercorn and St. Julian Streets. 025-192.)

THE OLIVER STURGES HOUSE

This house built in 1813 by Oliver Sturges, successful Savannah merchant, occupies the site of the parsonage of John Wesley, minister of the Church of England in Georgia 1736-37 and founder of Methodism.

Mr. Sturges was a two-fifths owner of the Steam Ship SAVANNAH, first steamship ever built and first to cross the Atlantic. The SAVANNAH'S historic voyage was planned in the Sturges House, which was one of a pair of brick Federal-style residences located on Trust Lot T, Reynolds Ward. Mr. Sturges' partner, Benjamin Burroughs, lived in the other residence, where the John Wesley Hotel is presently located.

Morris Newspaper Corporation, owner and operator of newspapers throughout the United States, purchased the Sturges House from Historic Savannah Foundation in 1971 for conversion into corporate headquarters. The careful restoration of the house was completed in 1973.

The Oliver Sturges House has been entered on the National Register of Historic Places.

(Located next to Reynolds Square at Abercorn and St. Julian Streets. 025-191.)

JOHNSON SQUARE

Johnson Square is named for Governor Robert Johnson of South Carolina who befriended the colonists when Georgia was first settled. It was laid out by Oglethorpe and by Colonel William Bull in 1733, and was the first of Savannah's squares. In early colonial days the public stores, the house for strangers, the church, and the public bake oven stood on the trust lots around it.

MAJOR GENERAL NATHANAEL GREENE
(1742-1786)

Events of historical interest are associated with Johnson Square. Here in
1735, Chekilli, head Chief of the
Creek Nation, recited the origin
myth of the Creeks. In 1737, the
Rev. John Wesley, after futile efforts
to bring to trial certain indictments
against him growing out of his ministry at Savannah, posted a public
notice in this Square that he intend-
ed to return to England. The Declaration of Independence was read
here to an enthusiastic audience,
August 10, 1776.

In 1819 a ball was given for President James Monroe in a pavilion
erected in the Square. Eminent men
who have spoken here include the
Marquis de LaFayette, (1825); Henry
Clay (1847); and Daniel Webster
(1848). Beneath the Nathanael
Greene monument rest the remains
of the famous Revolutionary general
and his son.

(Located in Johnson Square at Bull
and St. Julian Streets. GHM 025-
38A, 1955.)

THE NATHANAEL GREENE MONUMENT

NATHANAEL GREENE MONUMENT

Beneath the monument in this
Square repose the remains of Maj.
Gen. Nathanael Greene, of Rhode
Island, who died near Savannah on
June 19, 1786, at Mulberry Grove
Plantation which had been granted
to him by this State in appreciation
of his services in the Revolution.

The 50 foot, white marble obelisk,
designed by the well-known
architect, William Strickland, was
completed in 1830. The original cornerstone was laid here on March 21,

TELFAIR ACADEMY

1825, by Greene's old friend, the Marquis de Lafayette. At the dedicatory ceremony General Lafayette said: "The great and good man to whose memory we are paying a tribute of respect, affection, and regret, has acted in our revolutionary contest a part so glorious and so important that in the very name of Greene are remembered, all the virtues and talents which can illustrate the patriot, the statesman, and the military leader..."

General Greene's remains were originally interred in the burial ground now known as Colonial Cemetery. His exact resting place was a matter of doubt and speculation for many years. The remains of the famed Revolutionary hero were found in the Graham vault in 1901, and were reinterred beneath this monument the following year.

(Located in Johnson Square at Bull and St. Julian Streets. GHM 025-12, 1953.)

TELFAIR ACADEMY OF ARTS & SCIENCES

Created under the Will of Miss Mary Telfair (c.1789-1875), the Telfair Academy of Arts & Sciences opened as the first public art museum in the Southeast with a preliminary private showing February 12, 1885.

After extensive remodeling and additions with Detlef Lienau of New York as architect, the building was formally dedicated May 3, 1886.

MARY TELFAIR (C.1789-1875)

Among the prominent persons who attended the dedication were: Jefferson Davis and his daughter Winnie Davis; Charles C. Jones historian; Gen. A. R. Lawton; Gen. Henry R. Jackson; Gen. G. Moxley Sorrel; Col. John Screven and Col. Charles Olmstead.

Carl L. Brandt, N.A., served as Telfair's first Director, 1883-1905.

(Located next to Telfair Square at Barnard and State Streets. GHM 025-38B, 1956.)

TELFAIR FAMILY MANSION
(1818 – WILLIAM JAY, ARCHITECT)

This building is one of the city's outstanding examples of Regency architecture. The main floor and basement kitchens are maintained as a historic house museum. The rotunda and west wing are later additions. It was left by Savannah's outstanding philanthropist, Mary Telfair (1789-1875), relative of William Gibbons, friend of Peter Cooper, last surviving child of Edward Telfair (Revolutionary patriot and early Governor of Georgia) to house the Telfair Academy of Arts and Sciences which was founded under her will. Notable among her other public bequests are the Telfair Hospital, the interiors of the Independent Presbyterian Church, and (with her sister) Hodgson Hall.

In the Colonial and Revolutionary periods "Government house," the residence of the Royal Governors of Georgia, stood on this site. Here on the night of January 18, 1776, in one of the dramatic episodes of the American Revolution, Major Joseph Habersham, commanding a small force of patriots, walked alone into the chamber where Governor Wright was conferring with his Council and announced, "Sir James, you are my prisoner." Habersham later became Postmaster-General of the United States.

(Located next to Telfair Square at Barnard and President Streets. GHM 025-28, 1954.)

TRINITY METHODIST CHURCH
MOTHER CHURCH OF SAVANNAH METHODISM

Trinity Church is the oldest Methodist Church in a city whose intimate association with John Wesley and George Whitefield gives it a unique place in the history of Methodism.

The cornerstone of the building was laid February 14, 1848, in a ceremony presided over by the Reverend Alfred T. Mann, Pastor. The edifice, which was completed in 1850, is in the Corinthian order of architecture and was designed by John B. Hogg of Savannah.

Prior to the erection of Trinity Church the Methodist congregation in Savannah worshiped in Wesley Chapel on South Broad Street. Among the great preachers of the Methodist Church whose names are associated with the Chapel are Francis Asbury, William Capers, John Howard, James C. Andrew, Ignatius Few, Elijah Sinclair and George F.

Pierce. Through their faith and service others have lived more valiantly.

(Located next to Telfair Square at Barnard and President Streets. GHM 025-67, 1958.)

LUTHERAN CHURCH OF THE ASCENSION
(FOUNDED, 1741)

On April 14, 1741, John Martin Bolzius, who as Pastor of the Salzburgers at Ebenezer was in charge of Lutheran work in the colony of Georgia, founded the congregation now known as the Lutheran Church of the Ascension.

In 1756 members of the congregation purchased for one hundred and fifty pounds the lot upon which the present church building stands, directly East of this marker. Around 1772 a nearby building which had formerly served as a court house was acquired at a cost of seventeen pounds and was moved to this site, becoming the first church building of Lutherans in Savannah.

The present church was erected in 1843. Extensive remodeling was completed in 1879 and at that time it was dedicated as "The Evangelical Lutheran Church of the Ascension." The choice of the name is connected with the beautiful stained glass window behind the altar, portraying the Ascension of Christ into heaven.

(Located in Wright Square at Bull and President Streets. GHM 025-76, 1960.)

TOMO-CHI-CHI'S BOULDER

TOMO-CHI-CHI'S GRAVE

Tomo-Chi-Chi, Mico of the Yamacraws, a tribe of the Creek Indian Nation, is buried in this Square. He has been called a co-founder, with Oglethorpe, of Georgia. He was a good friend to the English, a friendship indispensible to the establishment of the Colony as a military outpost against Spanish invasion. He negotiated with Oglethorpe the treaty, formally ratified on May 21, 1733, pursuant to which Georgia was settled. Mary Musgrove, half-breed niece of Emperor Brim of the Creek Indians, acted as interpreter between Oglethorpe and Tomo-Chi-Chi and lent her great influence to the signing of that treaty and to the treaties negotiated by Oglethorpe with other tribes of the Creek nation.

In 1734, at the age of 84, with his wife, Senauki Tomo-Chi-Chi visited the English Court and was received by the King and by the Archbishop of Canterbury. He was a man of fine physique, tall and of great dignity.

He died October 5, 1739 at Yamacraw Indian Village and at his request was brought to Savannah

COURTESY, UNIVERSITY OF GEORGIA LIBRARIES

TOMO-CHI-CHI AND HIS NEPHEW TOONAHOWI

COURTESY, GEORGIA DEPARTMENT OF ARCHIVES AND HISTORY

SIR JAMES WRIGHT (1716-1785)

to rest among his English friends. He was buried here with military honors.

(Located in Wright Square at Bull and President Streets. GHM 025-4, 1952.) **Note:** According to some sources Tomo-chi-chi, was born c. 1650 and died in 1737.

WRIGHT SQUARE

This Square, which was laid out in 1733, was originally named for John Percival, Earl of Egmont, who played a large part in founding the colony of Georgia. Its name was changed around 1763 to Wright Square in honor of James Wright, royal governor of the province of Georgia (1760-1782).

In the Town Hall which was located on the present site of the Chatham

County courthouse George Whitefield, Church of England minister at Savannah, preached to large congregations in early colonial days.

In 1739 Tomo-chi-chi, the Chief of the Yamacraw Indians who befriended the early Georgia colonists, was buried with ceremony in the center of this Square, Gen. Oglethorpe acting as one of the pallbearers.

The monument to William Washington Gordon (1796-1842) commemorates the founder and first president of Georgia's earliest railroad, the Central Railroad and Banking Company – an enterprise which greatly promoted the economy of this State. Designed by the distinguished architects, Henry Van Brunt and Frank M. Howe, the handsome monument to Gordon symbolizes the progress and prosperity of the world by means of

GORDON MONUMENT, WRIGHT SQUARE

MICHAEL HIPPLE

OWENS-THOMAS HOUSE

commerce, manufacture, agriculture, and art. It was completed in 1883.

(Located in Wright Square at Bull and President Streets. GHM 025-69, 1958.)

OWENS - THOMAS HOUSE
MARQUIS DE LAFAYETTE

This residence is the outstanding monument to the architectural genius of William Jay who completed his designs for its construction prior to his twenty-first birthday. Supervision of the work brought Jay to America in 1817. Its period is English Regency. Its style is known as Greek Revival. Its interiors are particularly notable and, in many features unique. Of its style and period it is Savannah's finest and among the nation's best.

The mansion was built 1816-1819 for Richard Richardson, a Savannah merchant. The basement, of "tabby" construction, is of much earlier date and contains the original trim of the de Brahm house which once occupied the site.

General LaFayette was quartered here as a guest of the City when he visited Savannah in 1825. He addressed the populace from the south balcony.

The mansion was left in trust to the Telfair Academy of Arts and Sciences in 1951 by Margaret Gray Thomas whose grandfather George W. Owens, distinguished lawyer and Member of Congress, acquired the property from the Bank of the United States. It is now a historic house museum.

(Located across from Oglethorpe Square at Abercorn and President Streets. GHM 025-26, 1954.)

DAVENPORT HOUSE

COLONIAL TOWN GATE DAVENPORT HOUSE

In 1757, during the administration of royal Governor Henry Ellis, a line of earthwork defenses, including a palisade, was erected around Savannah. Immediately west of this marker was located Bethesda Gate, one of the six entrances into the town. Through Bethesda Gate passed the Sea Island Road connecting Savannah and the tidewater settlements to the east and southeast.

This square, known as Columbia Square, was laid out in 1799. Facing it on the north is the "Davenport House," one of the handsomest examples of Georgian architecture in the South. This finely proportioned dwelling, completed in 1820, was designed and built by its owner, Isaiah Davenport (1784-1827), one of Savannah's outstanding builder-architects.

In 1956 the "Davenport House" was restored by Historic Savannah Foun-

dation as the first preservation project of that organization. It is open to the public at certain times during the week.

(Located in Columbia Square at Habersham and President Streets. GHM 025-75, 1959.)

1812 WESLEY CHAPEL

Savannah Methodism's first church building was erected on this corner of Lincoln and South Broad (now Oglethorpe) streets in 1812 by its first pastor, Rev. James Russell.

Bishop Francis Asbury preached twice in Wesley Chapel on November 21, 1813. In 1819-20 under the preaching of William Capers the membership grew rapidly, and in 1821 John Howard enlarged the building to care for 100 new members. By 1848 this "good, neat house, sixty by forty feet," became too small; at a new location its successor, Trinity, was built. Among the early pastors of Wesley Chapel were James O. Andrew, George F. Pierce, Ignatius A. Few, and Thomas L. Wynn.

(Located at Oglethorpe Avenue and Lincoln Street. MHS 025-182, 1977.)

CONRAD AIKEN

Conrad Aiken, Poet and Man of Letters, was born in Savannah on August 5, 1889, and lived at No. 228 (opposite) until 1901. After the tragic death of his parents, he was moved

COURTESY, THE ACADEMY OF AMERICAN POETS

CONRAD AIKEN (1889-1973)

to New England. Most of his writing career was divided between Cape Cod, Massachusetts and Rye, England. In 1962 he returned to Savannah to live and write in the adjoining house, No. 230 until his death August 17, 1973. Of his home here he wrote,: "Born in that most magical of cities, Savannah, I was allowed to run wild in that earthly paradise until I was nine; ideal for the boy who early decided he wanted to write."

Though he wrote novels, short stories and critical essays, his first love was poetry. His work earned many awards including the Pulitzer Prize (1930), National Book Award (1954), and the National Medal of Literature (1969). He was a member of the National Academy of Arts and Sciences and held the Chair of Poetry of the Library of Congress (1950 to 1952). Governor Jimmy Carter

appointed him Poet Laureate of Georgia on March 30, 1973. Conrad Aiken is buried beside his parents in Bonaventure Cemetery.

(Located on Oglethorpe Avenue across from Colonial Park Cemetery. GHS/HSF 025-183, 1980.)

COLONIAL PARK

This cemetery, the second in colonial Savannah, was the burying ground for the city from about 1750 until it was closed against burials in 1853.

Among the distinguished dead who rest here are Archibald Bulloch, first President of Georgia; James Habersham, acting royal Governor of the Providence, 1771-73; Joseph Habersham, Postmaster General under three Presidents; Lachlan McIntosh, Major General, Continental Army; Samuel Elbert, Revolutionary soldier and Governor of Georgia; Capt. Denis L. Cottineau de Kerloguen who aided John Paul Jones in the engagement between the "Bon Homme Richard" and the "Serapis"; Hugh McCall, early historian of Georgia; Edward Greene Malbone, the noted miniaturist, and Colonel John S. McIntosh, a hero of the War with Mexico.

The remains of Major General Nathanael Greene who died in 1786 reposed in the Graham vault until they were reinterred in 1901 in Johnson Square.

The cemetery became a city park in 1896.

COLONIAL PARK CEMETERY

(Located at the entrance to Colonial Park Cemetery, Abercorn Street and Oglethorpe Avenue. GHM 025-20, 1954.)

OLD COLONIAL CEMETERY 1733

Established in earliest colonial days. Vested in Christ Church 1758. Closed in 1853. Transferred to city and made park in 1895. Illustrious men of 120 years rest here.

(Located at the entrance to Colonial Park Cemetery, Abercorn Street and Oglethorpe Avenue. ACH 025-188, 1930.) ♦ ★ – not standing.

COL. JAMES S. McINTOSH (1784-1847)

James S. McIntosh achieved an immortal record of gallantry in the War of 1812 and in the War with Mexico. In 1814 he saw considerable action on the Canadian border being severely wounded at Buffalo. In the Mexican War, Col. McIntosh was desperately wounded by bayonets at Resaca de la Palma in 1846. When a fellow officer, who found him on the field, asked if he might be of any service McIntosh replied, "Yes, give me some water and show me my regiment." Returning to combat the following year despite his wounds and advanced years, the brave Georgian was mortally wounded while leading his brigade at the bloody storming of El Molino del Rey, Sept. 8, 1847. His remains were brought home by the State of Georgia in 1848 and were reinterred in the McIntosh vault with military honors.

A native of Liberty County, McIntosh was one of the "fighting McIntoshes" who illustrated their country on many battle-fields. He was the great nephew of Lachlan McIntosh and his father was the Revolutionary hero, John McIntosh, who when the British demanded the surrender of Fort Morris at Sunbury sent back the defiant answer: "Come and take it." Col. James S. McIntosh's son, James McQueen McIntosh, became a general in the Confederate Army and was killed in Arkansas while another son, John Baillie McIntosh, served the Union cause well, losing a leg at Winchester.

(Located in Colonial Park Cemetery, Abercorn Street and Oglethorpe Avenue. GHM 025-32, 1954.)

GEN. LACHLAN McINTOSH (1727-1806)

Lachlan McIntosh, Georgia's ranking Continental officer in the American Revolution, was the son of John Mor Mackintosh who settled with a group of Highlanders on the Altamaha in 1736. Lachlan served as a cadet in Oglethorpe's Regiment and received part of his schooling at Bethesda. During the Colonial era he became a leading planter at Darien, accumulating a considerable property which he lost in the Revolution.

A firm supporter of American rights, McIntosh was commissioned colonel of the first Continental regiment

COURTESY, GEORGIA HISTORICAL SOCIETY

GEN. LACHLAN McINTOSH (1727-1806)

raised in Georgia. A feud with Button Gwinnett, Signer of the Declaration of Independence, resulted in a duel fought near Savannah, May 16, 1777. McIntosh was transferred to Gen. Washington's headquarters after Gwinnett's death. He served with credit at Valley Forge and Washington, who described him as an "Officer of great worth and merit," later gave him command of the Western Department at Fort Pitt. Returning to Georgia in 1779, Gen. McIntosh took part in the Siege of Savannah. His military career in the American Revolution, in which he had shed his blood defending Georgia's borders, terminated with his capture when Charlestown fell in 1780.

In 1784 the Continental Congress promoted McIntosh to major general, vindicating him from his unjust suspension from command four years before as a result of representations to it by Gov. Walton. The patriot-hero lived out his remaining years at Savannah.

(Located in Colonial Park Cemetery, Abercorn Street and Oglethorpe Avenue. GHM 025-30, 1954.)

CAPT. DENIS N. COTTINEAU (1745-1808)

This grave links Savannah with one of history's greatest naval dramas – the epic fight in 1779 between the "Bon Homme Richard" and "Serapis" in which John Paul Jones immortalized himself.

Denis Nicolas Cottineau de Kerloguen received a commission in the Continental navy during the American Revolution. Commanding the slow sailing "Pallas" during the famous naval engagement of Sept. 23, 1779, Capt. Cottineau, by skillful seamanship, forced H.M.S. "Countess of Scarborough" to strike her colors. He was subsequently wounded in a dual with another officer, Pierre Landais, against whom Commodore Jones made serious charges after the battle.

Cottineau later settled in the French West Indies. During the slave insurrection in San Domingo he fled to Pennsylvania where he joined several fellow French refugees in establishing a colony. Suffering from a "lingering illness," he came to Savannah early in 1808. Capt. Cottineau died here, Nov. 29 of that year, at the residence of the Abbe Carles. Cottineau's widow was the sister of the Marquis de Montalet

who once owned the Hermitage plantation near Savannah.

In 1928 Ambassador Paul Claudel of France knelt in homage here at the grave of the gallant Frenchman who helped establish the prestige of the infant American navy.

(Located in Colonial Park Cemetery, Abercorn Street and Oglethorpe Avenue. GHM 025-55, 1957.)

HUGH McCALL (1767-1823)
EARLY GEORGIAN HISTORIAN

Hugh McCall who is buried here was the author of the first history of Georgia.

Forced by ill health into retirement, McCall, who was a brevet major, U.S. Infantry, became interested in the history of his adopted State. In spite of severe handicaps, he wrote a much needed history of Georgia. The first volume was published at Savannah, in 1811. The second volume, which appeared five years later, carried his "History of Georgia" through the Revolutionary period. Time has not impaired the value and the usefulness of McCall's work.

His father, Colonel James McCall, played a heroic role in the Revolutionary War in the Carolinas. Hugh McCall passed his boyhood during those trying times. The closing words of the first history of this State are an ever timely reminder to posterity that "The blood which flowed from the suffering patriots of that day, should never be forgotten;

and the precious jewel which was purchased by it, should be preserved with courage and remembered with gratitude, by succeeding generations."

(Located in Colonial Park Cemetery, Abercorn Street and Oglethorpe Avenue. GHM 025-24, 1954.)

EDWARD GREENE MALBONE
(1777-1807)

Beneath this modest slab rest the remains of America's foremost painter of miniatures.

Malbone, a native of Rhode Island, began his career in Providence at the age of seventeen. He pursued his calling in Boston, New York, Philadelphia, Charleston and in London, England.

Exacting and unceasing work undermined his constitution. Having sought in vain to recover his health in the island of Jamaica, he came to Savannah in fore-knowledge of death and died here in the home of his cousin, Robert Mackay, on May 7, 1807.

Though not yet thirty years of age when he died, he left no peer in his art. Time has justified the statements you may read here in his epitaph. Today Malbone is acknowledged to be the finest miniaturist his country has yet produced, and among the greatest of all time anywhere.

(Located in Colonial Park Cemetery, Abercorn Street and Oglethorpe Avenue. GHM 025-21, 1954.)

WILLIAM STEPHENS
FIRST GRAND MASTER,
GRAND LODGE OF GEORGIA, F.&A.M.

Born Jan. 1752 at Beaulieu (Bulie) near Savannah of distinguished English ancestry William Stephens was an eminent lawyer and jurist during and after the War for Independence.

Georgia's first Attorney-General, he was also Chief Justice of Georgia, Mayor of Savannah and held other important posts of honor. In 1802 President Thomas Jefferson appointed him United States District Court Judge which position he held with distinction until just prior to his death on 6 Aug. 1819.

A dedicated freemason, he was Worshipful Master of Solomon's Lodge at Savannah prior to 1783. In 1791 he was Worhipful Master of another Savannah Lodge, Union No. 10 (extinct).

When the Grand Lodge of Georgia F.&A.M., was organized at Savannah on 16 Dec. 1786 as the independent and sovereign Masonic power in Georgia, William Stephens was elected Grand Master and he served through 1788. In 1793 he was re-elected Grand Master and served continuously through 1813. A record of longevity in that exalted Masonic office never since equalled.

The honored remains of Grand Master Stephens rest in the Colonial Cemetery of Savannah. His Masonic posterity, the nearly 100,000 freemasons of Georgia will ever cherish his memory.

(Located in Colonial Park Cemetery, Abercorn Street and Oglethorpe Avenue. GLG 025-187, 1970.)

GEN. SAMUEL ELBERT
(1740-1788)

Samuel Elbert, who became brigadier general in the Continental Army and Governor of Georgia, migrated to this Province from South Carolina as an orphan youth during the Colonial period. He prospered in mercantile pursuits and as an Indian trader; became a member of the Commons House of Assembly from Ebenezer, and was captain of a grenadier company prior to the Revolution. A staunch patriot, Elbert served on the Council of Safety and in the first Provincial Congress of Georgia in 1775. He was commissioned (1776) lieut-colonel of the first Continental regiment raised here. Col. Elbert participated in two Florida expeditions; gallantly commanded the Georgia Line at the fall of Savannah (1778); was captured by the British at Briar Creek (1779) and later took part in the Yorktown campaign. He was promoted to brig. general in the Continental Army in 1783. He became Governor of this State, Sheriff of Chatham County and Grand Master of Georgia Masons.

Elbert died Nov. 2, 1788, and was buried at Rae's Hall Plantation near Savannah. In time, the burial place of the Revolutionary hero was forsaken and forgotten. During the early years of the 20th century the grave was desecrated and exposed when earth was removed from the

COURTESY, GEORGIA DEPARTMENT OF ARCHIVES AND HISTORY

COLONEL SAMUEL ELBERT
LEADER OF THE CONTINENTAL ARMY IN GEORGIA

Indian mound on which he and his wife, Elizabeth Rae Elbert, were buried. Following identification by acceptable evidence the remains of the Revolutionary hero were rescued in 1916 by a committee of the Sons of the Revolution, headed by R.J. Travis. The bones of the patriot were reinterred here in 1924 with full military honors.

(Located in Colonial Park Cemetery, Abercorn Street and Oglethorpe Avenue. GHM 025-29, 1954.)

JOSEPH HABERSHAM
(1751-1815)
JOHN HABERSHAM
(1754-1799)
JAMES HABERSHAM, JR.
(1745-1799)

The three Habersham brothers – who here rest beside their distinguished father, James Habersham –

were prominent patriots in the American Revolution and outstanding public men during the early years of the Republic.

JOSEPH HABERSHAM, ardent Son of Liberty and a member of the Council of Safety, took part in the raid on the King's powder magazine in 1775, and in 1776 personally accomplished the dramatic arrest of the Royal Governor, Sir James Wright. He served in the Revolution as a Lieut. Col. in the Ga. Continental line; was twice Speaker of the General Assembly; Mayor of Savannah, 1792-93; and Postmaster General of the U.S., 1795-1801.

JOHN HABERSHAM, Major in the first Ga. Continental Regt., distinguished himself in the Revolutionary War during which he was twice taken prisoner. He was a member of the Continental Congress in 1785; Commissioner in the Convention which established the Ga.-S.C. boundary; and first Collector of Customs at Savannah.

JAMES HABERSHAM, JR., merchant, actively opposed the revenue acts of Parliament in 1775. He served (as did John Habersham) on the Board of Trustees created in 1785 to establish the University of Georgia, and was Speaker of the General Assembly in 1782 and 1784.

(Located in Colonial Park Cemetery, Abercorn Street and Oglethorpe Avenue. GHM 025-14, 1953.)

COURTESY, GEORGIA HISTORICAL SOCIETY

JAMES HABERSHAM (1715-1775)

JAMES HABERSHAM

Here rests James Habersham – associate of George Whitefield and a leading merchant, planter, and public servant during Georgia's colonial era.

Mr. Habersham came to the colony in 1738 as a youthful follower of the Rev. Whitefield and collaborated with that eminent divine in the founding of Bethesda orphanage. He successfully administered the affairs of that institution during its early years. He established, in 1744, what developed into the most important commercial house in the Province, and became one of Georgia's largest planters.

During the colonial period he ably filled a number of important public positions, including provincial

Secretary; President of His Majesty's Council for Georgia, and acting Governor of the Province during the absence of Sir James Wright, 1771-1773.

Though he disapproved Parliament's oppressive acts, Habersham remained firmly loyal to the Crown. Universally respected, he died, while visiting in New Jersey, August 28, 1775 – his last days darkened by the shadow of the impending Revolutionary struggle which arrayed, in his words and in his own case, "father against son, and son against father."

(Located in Colonial Park Cemetery, Abercorn Street and Oglethorpe Avenue. GHM 025-15, 1953.)

JOSEPH CLAY, PATRIOT

A native of Yorkshire, Joseph Clay (1741-1804) settled at Savannah at the age of nineteen. His uncle, James Habersham, declared that his "Industry" was "highly commendable" and "his Abilities for Trade unquestionable." Fulfilling his early promise, Clay prospered in Georgia as a merchant and rice planter.

He was a staunch supporter of American rights, served on the Council of Safety and in the Provincial Congress and took part in the celebrated raid on the Royal powder magazine at Savannah in 1775. During the Revolutionary War Clay rendered efficient and faithful service to the American cause as a deputy paymaster general of the Continental Army for the Southern Department. His career in the Revolution was dis-

tinguished by "Virtue & fortitude," said General James Jackson, who also paid high tribute to Clay's wife Ann (whose remains also lie here) for her beneficent care of the American wounded after the Battle of Camden.

In the years following the Revolution Joseph Clay held several positions of importance, including state treasurer and judge of the inferior court. He was one of the first trustees for the state college that later became the University of Georgia. He died Dec. 15, 1804. Joseph Clay's published letters (1776-1793) constitute a valuable historical source work for the period.

(Located in Colonial Park Cemetery, Abercorn Street and Oglethorpe Avenue. GHM 025-50, 1957.)

ARCHIBALD BULLOCH

"This is no time to talk of moderation; in the present instance it ceases to be a virtue."

– Speech to Provincial Congress, June 5, 1776.

Foremost among Georgia's Revolutionary patriots stood Archibald Bulloch whose remains rest in this vault. An early and staunch advocate of American rights, Bulloch was among the patriots who issued the call in 1774 for the first province-wide meeting of the friends of Liberty in Georgia.

He served as President of the 1st and the 2nd Provincial Congress & was a

COURTESY, GEORGIA DEPARTMENT OF ARCHIVES AND HISTORY

ARCHIBALD BULLOCH (1730-1777)

delegate in 1775 to the Continental Congress where he won John Adams' praise for his "abilities and fortitude."

In April, 1776, Mr. Bulloch became the first President and Commander in Chief of Georgia, an office he ably filled until his untimely death during the latter part of February, 1777. His loss was a severe blow to the revolutionary cause in Georgia as his was the only leadership which united the Whig factions in the troubled young State.

Theodore Roosevelt was the great-great-grandson of the Georgia patriot.

(Located in Colonial Park Cemetery, Abercorn Street and Oglethorpe Avenue. GHM 025-17B, 1953.)

MAJOR JOHN BERRIEN
(1759-1815)

In 1775 John Berrien of New Jersey came to the province of Georgia, where one of his mother's kin had previously settled. His father John Berrien (1711-1772), was a judge of the supreme court of New Jersey and a trustee of Princeton College. From the Berrien home at Rock Hill, N. J., General Washington issued his farewell address to the army in 1783.

At the age of 17 John Berrien was commissioned 2nd Lieutenant in the first Georgia Continental brigade (1776). A few months later he was promoted to 1st Lieutenant and the following year he was commissioned captain. A firm supporter of General Lachlan McIntosh in the troubles that befell that officer after his slaying of Button Gwinnett in a duel, Berrien followed McIntosh to Washington's headquarters in 1777 and served as brigade major of the North Carolina troops at Valley Forge.

After the Revolution Berrien returned to Georgia with his family, which included his young son, John MacPherson Berrien, who was destined to become one of Georgia's most illustrious statesmen. Active in public life in Georgia, Major John Berrien was for several years Collector of Customs at Savannah; served as an alderman, and was State Treasurer at Louisville (1796-1799). Berrien died at Savannah on November 6, 1815.

(Located in Colonial Park Cemetery, Abercorn Street and Oglethorpe Avenue. GHM 025-49, 1957.)

NATHANAEL GREENE,
MAJ. GEN., CONTINENTAL ARMY
JOHN MAITLAND,
LT. COL., 71ST REGT.
OF SCOTCH FOOT

This tomb, known as the Graham vault, possesses the distinction of having been the burial place of two heroes of the Revolutionary War, one American and the other British.

Lt. Col. John Maitland of Lauder, Scotland, son of the 6th Earl of Lauderdale, won wide acclaim for his feat in bringing 800 Highlanders and Hessian troops by water from Beaufort to Savannah in Sept. 1779, under the eyes of the French fleet. The timely arrival of these reinforcements enabled Gen. Prevost to defend Savannah against the besieging French and American forces.

Maitland died at Savannah on October 26, 1779, shortly after the siege was raised. The British hero was buried in the vault of the Royalist Lieutenant Governor, John Graham. Col. Maitland's remains were, apparently, removed later to another burial place.

Nathanael Greene of Rhode Island, one of Washington's most brilliant generals, who died on June 19, 1786, at Mulberry Grove near Savannah, was also interred in the Graham vault. His burial place later became the subject of conjecture and remained so until 1901 when this tomb was opened and his remains identified. Gen. Greene's ashes now repose beneath his monument in Johnson Square.

COURTESY, GEORGIA DEPARTMENT OF ARCHIVES AND HISTORY

NATHANAEL GREENE (1742-1786)

(Located in Colonial Park Cemetery, Abercorn Street and Oglethorpe Avenue. GHM 025-11, 1952.)

GREAT YELLOW FEVER EPIDEMIC OF 1820

In this cemetery many victims of the Great Yellow Fever Epidemic of 1820 were buried. Nearly 700 Savannahians died that year, including two local physicians who lost their lives caring for the stricken.

Several epidemics followed. In 1854 The Savannah Benevolent Association was organized to aid the families of the fever victims.

(Located in Colonial Park Cemetery, Abercorn Street and Oglethorpe Avenue. TGC 025-186, 1870.)

JAMES JOHNSTON
GEORGIA'S FIRST
NEWSPAPER PUBLISHER & PRINTER

Here repose the remains of James Johnston (1738-1808) – editor of Georgia's first newspaper.

A native of Scotland, Johnston settled at Savannah in 1761. "Recommended as a person regularly bred to and well skilled in the Art and mystery of Printing," he was appointed public printer of the Province by legislative Act during the following year. The first issue of the GEORGIA GAZETTE appeared at Savannah on April 7, 1763, and with some interruptions publication continued until 1802.

In the American Revolution Johnston sympathized with the royal government and, in his words "refused to admit to his Paper any of the Seditious publications then circulating thro' the different provinces." He closed his printing press in February, 1776. When British rule was restored in 1779 he returned to Savannah and resumed publication of the newspaper under the title, ROYAL GEORGIA GAZETTE.

A good man and a skilled printer, Johnston did not lose the respect of the Patriots. After the Revolution he was permitted to return. In 1783 he began publication again under the style, GAZETTE OF THE STATE OF GEORGIA. He died in his 70th year, October 4, 1808.

(Located in Colonial Park Cemetery, Abercorn Street and Oglethorpe Avenue. GHM 025-37, 1955.)

DUELLIST'S GRAVE

The epitaph to James Wilde on the nearby tomb is a melancholy reminder of the days of duelling and, particularly, of a tragic affair of honor fought January 16, 1815, on the Carolina side of the river near Savannah. Lieutenant Wilde was shot through the heart in a fourth exchange of fire by Captain Roswell P. Johnson, referred to in the epitaph, in bitterness, as "a man who a short time before would have been friendless but for him." The duellists were officers in the 8th Regt., U.S. Infantry. The nature of their quarrel is unknown.

Richard Henry Wilde, the poet and statesman, was the brother of the young officer. Lieutenant Wilde had served in the campaign against the Seminoles and his vivid descriptions of Florida suggested to the poet an epic poem, which, like the life of James Wilde, was cut short by the fatal bullet.

The unfinished poem is remembered for the beauty of a single lyric, the opening stanza of which is:

"My life is like the Summer Rose
  "That opens to the morning sky;
"But ere the shades of evening close
  "Is scattered on the ground – to die."

(Located in Colonial Park Cemetery, Abercorn Street and Oglethorpe Avenue. GHM 025-22, 1954.)

WILLIAM SCARBROUGH
PROMOTER OF THE FIRST
TRANSOCEANIC STEAMSHIP

William Scarbrough (1776-1838) was the moving force among the enterprising business men of Savannah who in 1819 sent the first steamship across the Atlantic Ocean. The corporate charter which Scarbrough and his associates obtained from the Georgia Legislature in 1818 recited that "they have formed themselves into an association, under the style and name of The Savannah Steam Ship Company, to attach, either as auxiliary or principal, the propulsion of steam to sea vessels, for the purpose of navigating the Atlantic and other oceans...."

The side-wheel steamship "Savannah," a vessel of 350 tons, was built in the North under specifications of Scarbrough and his business associates. She steamed from Savannah May 22, 1819, on her epoch-making voyage to Europe, reaching Liverpool 27 days later.

William Scarbrough was the son of a wealthy planter of the Beaufort District, S.C. Educated in Europe, he moved to Savannah about 1798 and soon attained a leading place in the life of the community, becoming one of Savannah's so-called "Merchant Princes" of the era. The handsome Scarbrough residence, which still stands on West Broad Street, was a center of the social life of the city. There William Scarbrough and his vibrant wife, Julia Bernard Scarbrough (1786-1851), entertained President James Monroe as a house guest in 1819.

(Located in Colonial Park Cemetery, Abercorn Street and Oglethorpe Avenue. GHM 025-44, 1957.)

JOSEPH VALLENCE BEVAN
(1798 - 1830)
GEORGIA'S FIRST OFFICIAL HISTORIAN

There was "None, No None!" reads the epitaph on this tomb, "Against Whose Name The Recording Angel Would More Reluctantly Have Written Down Condemnation."

Born at Dublin, Ireland, son of a Georgia planter, Joseph V. Bevan attended the Univ. of Georgia for two years and graduated in 1816 from the College of S. C. after which he enlarged his education in England. There he became the friend of the celebrated William Godwin who wrote the young Georgian a widely-published letter suggesting a course of studies.

In 1824 Bevan became the first official historian of Georgia. The Legislature empowered him to collect and publish the papers and documents in the State archives. This he did with method and industry and was the first to recognize the importance of copying the Colonial records of Georgia in London.

Bevan served Chatham County in the Legislature in 1827. A former editor of the Augusta *Chronicle*, he became in 1828 co-editor and co-publisher of the Savannah *Georgian*. His projected history of Georgia was never completed, death cutting short the career of the popular Savannahian at the age of thirty-two.

(Located in Colonial Park Cemetery, Abercorn Street and Oglethorpe Avenue. GHM 025-85, 1964.)

GEN. LACHLAN McINTOSH'S HOME 1782

First session of Georgia Legislature held here after evacuation of city by British in 1782. Washington visited house in 1789.

(Located at 110 East Oglethorpe Avenue near junction with Drayton Street. ACH 025-168, 1930.) ♦ ★ – not standing. **Note:** The house is standing.

LOWELL MASON (1792-1872)

Lowell Mason, noted composer of sacred music, was organist of the Independent Presbyterian Church (1820-1827) and Superintendent of its Sunday School (1815-1827).

A native of New England, Mason moved to Savannah at the age of twenty. He resided in this city for approximately fifteen years until his return to Massachusetts in 1827. He was active in the civic and religious life of his adopted city. He served as Secretary of the Savannah Missionary Society; and was an organizer of a school for the instruction of sacred music, and was Superintendent of the inter-denominational Savannah Sabbath School.

While Mason was the organist of the Independent Presbyterian Church, he set to music Bishop Reginald

Heber's hymn, "From Greenland's Icy Mountain." In the church that then stood on this site the now famous hymn was sung in 1824 for the first time.

Among later well known compositions by Mason was the music for the great hymns, "My Faith Looks Up to Thee" and "Nearer, My God, to Thee."

(Located at Bull Street and Oglethorpe Avenue. GHM 025-36, 1955.)

INDEPENDENT PRESBYTERIAN CHURCH

The Independent Presbyterian Church was organized in 1755. The first meeting house stood facing Market Square in Savannah, between what are now St. Julian and Bryan Streets, on property granted by King George II for the use and benefit of those dissenters who were professors of the doctrines of the Church of Scotland agreeable to the Westminster Confession of Faith.

The original church building erected on the present site was designed by John H. Greene, a gifted Rhode Island architect. In 1819 it was dedicated with impressive services which were attended by President James Monroe. The church was destroyed by fire in 1889.

The present church building was completed in 1891. The architect, William G. Preston, followed the general plan of the former structure. It is regarded as a notable example of American church architecture.

INDEPENDENT PRESBYTERIAN CHURCH
ORGANIZED IN 1755

Among the distinguished ministers of the Independent Presbyterian Church since its founding have been John Joachim Zubly, 1758-1781; Henry Kollock, 1806-1819; Daniel Baker, 1828-1831; Willard Preston, 1831-1856; and I.S.K. Axson, 1857-1891.

Ellen Louise Axson who was born in the manse of the Independent Presbyterian Church in 1860 was married in 1885 to Woodrow Wilson, later President of the United States, in a room in the manse.

(Located at Bull Street and Oglethorpe Avenue. GHM 025-35, 1955.)

JAMES MOORE WAYNE
(1790 - 1867)
FOR 32 YEARS ASSOCIATE JUSTICE OF THE U.S. SUPREME COURT

The residence opposite this site, known as the Gordon House, was built between 1819-1821. A fine example of Regency architecture, it was designed by the eminent architect, William Jay. The third story and side porch were later added.

The house was originally owned by James M. Wayne, one of Georgia's most illustrious public men. After service as Mayor of Savannah, Judge of the Eastern Circuit, and as Congressman, he was appointed to the Supreme Court of the United States by President Jackson in 1835. An able and courageous jurist, Wayne served on the highest court with distinction until his death in 1867 at Washington.

Though devoted to his native State, Judge Wayne was a strong Unionist. Opposing Secession, he remained on the Supreme Court after Georgia left the Union, a decision sharply contrasting with the course of his son, Henry C. Wayne, who resigned his commission in the U.S. Army in 1860 on the approach of war to serve Georgia as Adjutant General.

The Wayne residence was purchased in 1831 by a distinguished Savannahian, William Washington Gordon (1796-1842), organizer and first President of the Central of Georgia Railroad. President Taft was a guest there in 1909.

(Located at Bull Street and Oglethorpe Avenue. GHM 025-6, 1952.)

COURTESY, GIRL SCOUTS OF THE U.S.A.

JULIETTE GORDON LOW

BIRTHPLACE OF
JULIETTE LOW (1860 - 1927)
FOUNDER OF
THE GIRLS SCOUTS OF THE U.S.A.

In the house that stands opposite this marker Juliette Gordon Low, founder of the Girl Scouts of the United States of America, was born, October 31, 1860. It was her girl-hood home until her marriage there in 1886 to William Low, an English-man, then residing in Savannah.

As a friend of Lord Baden-Powell, founder of the Scout Movement, Juliette Low became active in Girl Guide work in England and Scotland in 1911. It was at his suggestion that she started Girl Scouting in America.

On March 12, 1912, at the Louisa Porter Home in this city, Mrs. Low founded the first Girl Guide troop in the United States. Her niece, Daisy Gordon, of Savannah, was the first

member enrolled. Through Mrs. Low's energetic and determined lead-ership the movement spread rapidly under the name "Girl Scouts." Mrs. Low died in Savannah, January 17, 1927. In 1953 her birthplace was acquired by the Girl Scouts of the United States of America, and funds for its restoration were raised by the 2,500,000 members. The property is now maintained by the Girl Scouts as a memorial to their Founder and as a center of activities for all Girl Scouts.

(Located at Bull Street and Ogle-thorpe Avenue. GHM 025-34, 1955.)

JAMES EDWARD OGLETHORPE
(1696 - 1785)

The monument in this Square to James Edward Oglethorpe – the great soldier-philanthropist who founded the colony of Georgia – was erected by the State of Georgia, the City of Savannah, and various Patriotic Societies. Impressive ceremonies marked its unveiling in 1910.

The 9 foot bronze statue of Ogle-thorpe is the work of one of America's foremost sculptors, the celebrated Daniel Chester French. He has depicted the Founder of Georgia in the full dress of a British general of the period. Oglethorpe is portrayed with sword in hand; alert and ready for council or action. At his feet is a palmetto frond. The statue faces southward symbolizing the threat of Spain's imperial ambitions to the young colony.

The pedestal and base of the monu-ment were designed by Henry

MONUMENT TO JAMES EDWARD OGLETHORPE
FOUNDER OF GEORGIA

DR. WM. A. CARUTHERS
(1802 - 46)
EARLY AMERICAN NOVELIST

One block west of this marker – at the northwest corner of Hull and Whitaker Streets – stood, formerly, the residence of William Alexander Caruthers, Virginia's earliest significant novelist. He resided in Savannah for several years before his death in 1846. Dr. Caruthers, who married Louisa Catherine Gibson of Whitemarsh Island, Chatham County, moved in 1837 to this city where he successfully practiced medicine. He took a prominent part in affairs in Savannah as a realtor; was one of the founders of the Georgia Historical Society and while an Alderman, 1841-1844, was instrumental in giving Savannahians direct election of their Mayors.

As one of the South's pioneering historical romancers, Caruthers rewrote and first published at Savannah his last and finest novel, "The Knights of the Golden Horse-Shoe" (1841), one of the earliest novels to be published in book form in Georgia. His first novel, "The Kentuckian in New-York" (1834), contains an admiring description of Savannah. Dr. Caruthers died of tuberculosis at Marietta, Ga. in 1846 and is buried there in an unlocated grave in St. James' churchyard.

(Located in Chippewa Square at Bull and McDonough Streets. GHM 025-31, 1954.) **Note:** The St. James Church has no record of Dr. Caruthers being buried in their cemetery.

Bacon, the eminent New York architect whose collaborations with Daniel Chester French include the Lincoln Memorial. The four lions at the corners of the lower base hold shields on which appear, respectively, the coat of arms of Oglethorpe and the great seals of the Colony of Georgia, the State, and the City of Savannah. On the pedestal of the monument is carved a portion of the text of the charter which was granted by Parliament in 1732 to "the Trustees for establishing the colony of Georgia in America."

(Located in Chippewa Square at Bull and McDonough Streets. GHM 025-45, 1957.)

COURTESY, GEORGIA HISTORICAL SOCIETY

COUNT CASIMIR PULASKI
POLISH PATRIOT WHO FOUGHT UNDER
GEORGE WASHINGTON

GENERAL CASIMIR PULASKI
SERGEANT WILLIAM JASPER

Near this spot two notable heroes of the American Revolution were mortally wounded in the ill-fated assault by the American and French forces upon the British lines here on October 9, 1779.

Brig. Gen. Casimir Pulaski, the famous Polish patriot, was fatally wounded by a grapeshot as he rode forward into the heavy fire from the British defenses located in this area.

Sergeant William Jasper fell a short distance west of this marker while attempting to plant the colors of the 2nd Regiment of South Carolina Continentals upon British entrenchments.

To their memory and to the memory of the hundreds of gallant soldiers of America and France – including the French commander-in-chief, Count d'Estaing – who shed their blood here in the cause of Liberty, this marker is erected.

(Located at West Broad and Liberty Streets at the Savannah Visitors Center. GHM 025-7, 1952.)

ATTACK ON BRITISH LINES
OCTOBER 9, 1779

Over this ground, hallowed by the valor and the sacrifices of the soldiery of America and of France, was fought, October 9, 1779, one of the bloodiest battles of the Revolution when Savannah, which the British had possessd for several months, was attacked by the combined American and French forces.

A short distance west of this marker stood the famous Spring Hill Redoubt and along here ran the line of entrenchments built by the British around Savannah. After a three weeks' siege, the Allies stormed the enemy works in this area on the early morning of October 9th.

Arrayed in the opposing armies that day were soldiers of many lands – American Continentals, Grenadiers of Old France, Irishmen in the service of King Louis XVI, Polish Lancers, French Creoles, and Negro volunteers from Haiti, fighting for American Independence against English Redcoats, Scotch Highlanders, Hessians, Royalist provincials from New York, Tory militia, armed slaves, and Cherokee Indians.

After an heroic effort to dislodge the British the Allies retired with heavy losses. Thus the siege was lifted, and the French fleet sailed from Georgia, ending an episode of far-reaching significance in the American Revolution.

(Located at West Broad and Liberty Streets at the Savannah Visitors Center. GHM 025-10, 1952.)

SPRINGHILL REDOUBT 1779

Keystone of British defenses in the assault on Savannah by French and American forces, October 9, 1779, when eleven hundred of the allied troops were killed or wounded, including Sergeant William Jasper and General Pulaski.

(Located at West Broad and Liberty Streets at the Savannah Visitors Center. ACH 025-179, 1930.) ♦ ★ – not standing.

ANDREW BRYAN

Andrew Bryan was born at Goose Creek, S.C. about 1716. He came to Savannah as a slave and here he was baptized by the Negro missionary, the Reverend George Leile, in 1781. Leile evacuated with the British in 1782 at the close of the American Revolution and Bryan took up his work. He preached at Yamacraw and at Brampton Plantation. On January 20, 1788, the Reverend Abraham Marshall (White) and the Reverend Jessie Peter (Colored) ordained Andrew Bryan and certified the congregation at a Brampton barn as the Ethiopian Church of Jesus Christ.

The Reverend Bryan moved from place to place with his congregation and was even imprisoned and whipped for preaching during a time when whites feared any slave gathering as a focus for rebellion. He persevered and finally bought his and his family's freedom and purchased this lot for his Church. Andrew Bryan pastored until his death, October 6, 1812. He is buried in Savannah's Laurel Grove Cemetery.

(Located at 575 West Bryan Street across from the Church. GHM 025-89, 1980.)

OLD JEWISH BURIAL GROUND

Established by Mordecai Sheftall on August 2, 1773 from lands granted him in 1762 by King George III as a parcel of land that "shall be, and forever remain, to and for the use and purpose of a Place of Burial for all persons whatever professing the Jewish Religion."

During the ill fated attempt of the French forces under Admiral Charles Henri, Comte d'Estaing, and the American forces under General Benjamin Lincoln, to recapture Savannah from the British, General Lincoln's Orders of the Day of October of October 8, 1779 stated that "The second place of rallying, or the first if the redoubt should not be carried, will be at the Jew's burying ground, where the reserve will be placed."

According to the account of Captain Antoine-Francoise Terance O'Connor, a military engineer serving with

The Old Jewish Burial Ground, Established August 2, 1773

the French forces, on October 9, 1779, shortly after 4:00 AM, "The reserve corps, commanded by M. le Vicomte de Noailles, advanced as far as an old Jewish cemetery, and we placed on its right and a little to the rear the four 4-pounders."

(Follow Jones Street west of West Broad Street 5 blocks, left on West Boundary Street, for 3 blocks, east on Cohen Street. Cemetery is off to the right. GHM/HCTF 025-180.) **Note:** Family burial ground of Levi Sheftall (1773) is about 100 yards away.

REVOLUTIONARY WAR
Barracks and Fortification

During the American Revolution the Military Barracks, which were located a short distance south of Savannah, stood here. Around this site heavy fighting took place in 1778 and 1779.

When Savannah was attacked by the British on December 29, 1778, a small contingent of Georgia Militia was stationed East of the barracks. Col. George Walton, a signer of the Declaration of Independence, was severely wounded near here while attempting to rally his militia, following a successful flanking movement by Sir Jas. Baird's light infantry around the right of the Continental line.

During the siege of Savannah in 1779 by French and American forces the brick barracks were dismantled by the British defenders who left standing only the lower portion of the South Wall. Under the direction of the famous British military engineer, Capt. James Montcrief, the remains of the barracks were converted into a strong fortification, known as a hornwork, which dominated the center of the Royalist lines around Savannah.

In 1834 the Federal Governor built military barracks, known as the Oglethorpe Barracks, on this site. They were razed in 1889 when the DeSoto Hotel was erected.

In 1965 the DeSoto Hotel was razed to make way for the DeSoto Hilton Hotel and the main office of the Citizens and Southern National Bank.

(Located at Bull and Liberty Streets in the DeSoto Hilton Plaza. GHM 025-09, 1952.)

OLD SORREL—WEED HOUSE

A fine example of Greek Revival style, this building (completed in 1840 from the plans of Charles B. Cluskey, a well-known Georgia architect) shows the distinguished trend of Savannah architecture during the first half of the 19th century. The Mediterranean villa influence reflects the French background of the original owner, Francis Sorrel (1793-1870), a shipping merchant of Savannah who as a child was saved by a faithful slave from the massacre of the white colonists in St. Domingo. The ante-bellum tradition of refinement and hospitality associated with the residence was continued after its purchase in 1859 by Henry D. Weed.

Here resided as a youth G. Moxley Sorrel (1838-1901) who achieved fame as one of "Lee's Lieutenants." Shortly after war broke out in 1861 Sorrel, a young bank clerk in Savannah, proceeded to Virginia where he obtained a place on Gen. Longstreet's staff. He served with conspicuous valor and zeal through the major battles and campaigns in that theater from the First Manassas to Petersburg and was thrice wounded. Sorrel became brig. general at the age of 26. Competent critics have called him "the best staff officer in the Confederate service." Gen. Sorrel's "Recollections of a Confederate Staff Officer" is an absorbing account of his war experiences.

(Located across from Madison Square at Bull and Macon Streets. GHM 025-27, 1954.)

MADISON SQUARE

Madison Square was laid out in 1839 and is named for the fourth president of the United States. Around the Square stand notable examples of the Greek revival, Gothic, and Romanesque architecture characteristic of nineteenth century Savannah.

To the west are St. John's Church (Episcopal), 1853, and the Green-Meldrim mansion, 1861, (Gen. W.T. Sherman's headquarters). To the north is the Francis Sorrel residence, 1840, which was visited by Gen. Robert E. Lee in 1862 when he commanded the Confederate coast defenses in this area. To the east is the Jewett house, erected 1842. The DeSoto Hotel and the Savannah

Volunteer Guards' Armory, of a later period, are in the Romanesque style typical of their designer, William G. Preston, of Boston.

The central bronze monument commemorates the heroism of Sergeant William Jasper (2nd Continental Regt. of South Carolina) who was mortally wounded, October 9, 1779, a short distance northwest of this marker, in the unsuccessful assault by the American and French forces upon the British lines, which ran immediately to the north of this Square.

(Located in Madison Square at Bull and Macon Streets. GHM 025-71, 1958.)

SERGEANT WILLIAM JASPER
HERO OF THE AMERICAN REVOLUTION

SERGEANT JASPER

Sergeant William Jasper, the famed Revolutionary hero, was mortally wounded a few hundred yards northwest of this spot on October 9, 1779, in the ill-fated attack of the American and French forces on the British defenses around Savannah. The monument to Jasper in this Square was unveiled in 1888 with great ceremony.

The 15$^1/_2$ foot bronze statue of Jasper was designed by the distinguished sculptor, Alexander Doyle of New York. The sculptor has depicted the heroic Sergeant bearing the colors of the Second Regiment of South Carolina Continentals during the assault at Savannah. His right hand, in which he holds a sabre, is pressed tight against the bullet wound in his side. Jasper's bullet-ridden hat lies at

his feet. His face, as portrayed by the sculptor, reveals intense suffering and resolute purpose.

The bas relief panels on the north, west and east sides of the monument represent the sculptor's conception of three episodes in Sergeant Jasper's Revolutionary career: – the ramparts of Fort Sullivan near Charleston where Jasper, under heavy fire, bravely replaced the flag; the liberation of Patriot prisoners by Jasper and a companion at what is now called Jasper Spring near Savannah; and the dying hero's last moments after the attack of October 9, 1779.

(Located in Madison Square at Bull and Macon Streets. GHM 025-47, 1957.)

THE HISTORIC GREEN-MELDRIM MANSION

SHERMAN'S HEADQUARTERS
GREEN-MELDRIM MANSION

General William Tecumseh Sherman used this house as headquarters from Dec. 22, 1864, until Feb. 1, 1865. Charles Green offered the use of his home to General Sherman and his staff. Sherman's chaplain conducted the Christmas services in St. John's Church.

The house was built for Green, a British subject, residing in Savannah prior to 1854. The architect was John S. Norris of New York. The house is notable as one of the country's finest examples of residential Gothic Revival architecture, the detail of the interiors being as sumptuous as any to be found in America. Cost of construction of this house in the 1850's totalled $93,000.

In 1892 it was acquired from the Green family as a residence by Judge Peter W. Meldrim, distinguished Georgia jurist and President of the American Bar Association (1912-1913).

St. John's Episcopal Church acquired the house from the Meldrim heirs in 1943 for use as a parish house and rectory. The house was purchased partly through public subscription by the citizens of Savannah. The house was declared a National Historic Landmark in 1976.

(Located across from Madison Square, at Bull and Macon Streets. GHM 025-5, 1980.)

SAVANNAH VOLUNTEER GUARDS
ORGANIZED 1802

As infantry the Corps fought in the War of 1812, Indian Wars and as a battalion in 1861, serving with distinction in defense of Savannah and Charleston. In the spring of 1864 joined Lee's Army at Petersburg. On April 3, 1865 serving in the rear guard on the retreat to Appomattox having been reduced to 85 men, 23 were killed, 35 wounded and remainder captured. Reorganized in 1872. Served as infantry battalion in the Spanish-American War, as a battalion of the 61 C.A.C. in WW-I, and as 118th F.A. Battalion in WW-II where they were awarded 5 Battle Stars. Reorganized after WWII and is now an active unit in the Georgia National Guard. This armory erected in 1892.

(Located near Madison Square, Bull and Carlton Streets. SVG 025-185, 1972.)

ANCIENT AND ACCEPTED SCOTTISH RITE OF FREEMASONRY
SAVANNAH, GEORGIA

The Scottish Rite of Freemasonry was introduced into Georgia in 1792 by Brother Abraham Jacobs. The first Degrees of the Rite of Perfection to be communicated in Savannah were on April 17, 1796, when Jacobs conferred the degrees on James Clark, Past Master, Solomon's Lodge No. 1, F.&A.M.

At Charleston, S.C., on May 31,

1801, the Supreme Council 33°, (Mother Council of the World) of the A.&A.S.R., S.J., U.S.A., was established.

On December 4, 1802, the Supreme Council, at Charleston, issued a Charter for the recently organized Lodge of Perfection 4°–14°, at Savannah, Georgia, and it was delivered in Savannah on December 30, 1802. Extant records indicate beyond reasonable doubt that this was the first such charter issued outside of Charleston.

Authorized and placed in 1969. Luther A. Smith, 33°, Sovereign Grand Commander; A. John Fulton, 33°, Sovereign Grand Inspector General. The Supreme Council 33°, A.&A.S.R., S.J., U.S.A.

(Located in Madison Square, at Bull and Macon Streets. GLG 025-184, 1969.)

FIRST GIRL SCOUT HEADQUARTERS IN AMERICA

The house adjacent to this building was the home of Juliette Gordon Low at the time she founded Girl Scouting in the United States, March 12, 1912. Formerly the carriage-house and stable of the Low mansion, this building became that year the first Girl Scout headquarters in America.

At the death of Mrs. Low in 1927 the Founder of Girl Scouts of the U.S.A. willed the original headquarters to the Girl Scouts of Savannah (now The Girl Scout Council of

COURTESY, GIRL SCOUTS OF THE U.S.A.

FIRST GIRL SCOUT HEADQUARTERS
FORMERLY THE CARRIAGE HOUSE AND STABLE
OF THE LOW MANSION

Savannah, Georgia, Inc.). This building has been continuously used for Girl Scouting longer than any other in this country.

(Located at Drayton and Macon Streets. GHM 025-87, 1966.)

"JINGLE BELLS"

James L. Pierpont (1822-1893), composer of "Jingle Bells," served as music director of this church in the 1850's when it was a Unitarian Church located on Oglethorpe Square. Son of the noted Boston reformer, Rev. John Pierpont, he was the brother of Rev. John Pierpont, Jr., minister of this church, and uncle of financier John Pierpont Morgan. He married Eliza Jane Purse, daughter of Savannah mayor Thomas Purse, and served with a Confederate cavalry regiment. He is buried in Laurel Grove Cemetery. A prolific song-writer, his best known "Jingle Bells" is world famous.

(Located across from Troup Square at Habersham and Macon Streets. 025-190, 1985.)

ST. VINCENT'S ACADEMY

The Convent and Academy of Saint Vincent dePaul was opened in June, 1845. Sisters of Mercy from Charleston, S.C., under the leadership of Mother Vincent Mahoney, began a boarding school, orphanage, day school and free school. St. Vincent's Convent became an independent Motherhouse within two years, and from here over 20 schools, hospitals, and orphanages were founded throughout Georgia. Early foundations continuing to give service include: St. Joseph's Hospital and St. Mary's Home, Savannah (1875), and St. Joseph's Hospital, Atlanta (1880).

Records attest to bravery and heroic service rendered by the Sisters of Mercy during the yellow fever epidemics of 1853, 1876, and 1878, and to their care for the wounded and suffering during the Civil War.

Students at St. Vincent's included Winnie and Jeff Davis, children of Confederate President Jefferson Davis.

Noted architect, Charles B. Cluskey, designed the Convent and Academy building. The style is Greek Revival.

Heritage Hall in the original building recalls for today's young women St. Vincent's tradition of educational excellence.

(Located at 207 East Liberty Street. GHM 025-93, 1983.)

CAPTURE OF SAVANNAH
DECEMBER 29, 1778

When the British attacked Savannah on December 29, 1778, the defending Continental forces, numbering about 650 men under command of Maj. Gen. Robert Howe, were posted across Sea Island Road (now Wheaton Street) approximately 100 yards east of this marker.

The British army, 2,500 strong, landed near Brewton Hill at daybreak on Dec. 29. It consisted of part of the 71st Highland Regiment, New York Loyalists, and Hessians, and was commanded by Lt. Col. Archibald Campbell. The British promptly marched on Savannah. They halted on the road about 800 yards from the American battle line and deployed for attack.

Col. Campbell meanwhile learned of an unguarded pass through the swamp, which led around the right of the American line. He thereupon detached the Light Infantry under Sir James Baird in an attempt, which proved successful, to flank the Continental position here.

Outflanked, the American position became untenable and Gen. Howe ordered Savannah evacuated. During the withdrawal, the Georgia Brigade, commanded by Gen. Lachlan McIntosh, was cut off and suffered heavy casualties.

During the subsequent siege of Savannah by the French and Americans in 1779 the British line of defenses around the Town ran through this area.

(Located at Liberty and Randolph Streets. GHM 025-8, 1952.)

MASSIE COMMON SCHOOL HOUSE
SAVANNAH'S CRADLE OF PUBLIC EDUCATION

Massie School is the only remaining building of Georgia's oldest chartered public school system. Constructed in 1855-56 and opened for classes on October 15, 1856, the Greek Revival building is listed on the National Register of Historic Places.

Peter Massie, a Scottish planter in Glynn County, Georgia, in 1841 bequeathed $5,000 "for the education of the poor children of Savannah." This donation was invested "until a large enough sum could be accumulated to build a school."

In 1855, the City retained John S. Norris to design and build Massie School. The center portion, costing $9,000 is the original structure. The west wing was built in 1872 from plans by John B. Hogg, and in 1886 the east wing was erected.

The building was used briefly as a hospital by federal troops after Sherman's occupation of Savannah in December, 1864. Beginning May 1, 1865, it was operated for a few months as a school for the Freedmen, with teachers from the American Missionary Association.

Massie School became a unit of the Savannah-Chatham County Board of Public Education when that body

COMER HOUSE, ERECTED ABOUT 1880

COURTESY, GEORGIA HISTORICAL SOCIETY

WINNIE DAVIS
"THE DAUGHTER OF THE CONFEDERACY"

was established in 1866. It was closed to regular classes in June, 1974, having educated Savannahians for 118 years.

(Located in Calhoun Square at Abercorn and Wayne Streets. GHM/BOE 025-189.)

COMER HOUSE
JEFFERSON DAVIS

Jefferson Davis, former President of the Confederate States of America, was a guest in 1886 in the house on the northeast corner of Bull and Taylor Streets. The residence (built about 1880) was at that time the home of Hugh M. Comer, President of the Central of Georgia Railway.

Accompanied by his daugher, Winnie Davis, "the Daughter of the Confederacy," Mr. Davis arrived in Savannah, May 3, 1886. He was escorted from Atlanta by a committee of Savannahians consisting of Hugh M. Comer, J. H. Estill, J. K.

Garnett, George A. Mercer, J. R. Saussy, and Gen. G. Moxley Sorrel. The trip to Savannah has been described as a "continuous ovation."

The occasion of the visit of Jefferson Davis was the celebration of the centennial of the Chatham Artillery, one of the oldest and most distinguished military units in the United States. During his stay in Savannah the former President of the Confederacy received tributes of respect and affection from the local citizenry, visiting military organizations as well as from the thousands of visitors who attended the centennial festivities.

(Located across from Monterey Square, at Bull and Taylor Streets. GHM 025-40, 1956.)

CASIMIR PULASKI

The great Polish patriot to whose memory this monument is erected was mortally wounded approximately one-half mile northwest of this spot during the assault by the French and American forces on the British lines around Savannah, October 9, 1779. General Pulaski was struck by a grapeshot as he rode forward, with customary ardor, from where his cavalry was stationed to rally the disorganized Allied columns. The fatal ball which was removed from his thigh by Dr. James Lynah of South Carolina is in possession of the Georgia Historical Society at Savannah.

Doubt and uncertainty exists as to where Pulaski died and as to his burial-place. A contemporary Charlestown, S.C. newspaper item and other sources indicate that he died aboard a ship bound for that port. It was generally believed that he was buried at sea.

A tradition persisted, however, that General Pulaski died at Greenwich plantation near Savannah and that he was buried there. When the monument here was under erection the grave at Greenwich was opened. The remains found there conformed, in the opinion of physicians, to a man of Pulaski's age and stature and were re-interred beneath this memorial in a metallic case in 1854.

(Located in Monterey Square at Bull and Wayne Streets. GHM 025-25, 1954.)

CONGREGATION MICKVE ISRAEL

CONGREGATION MICKVE ISRAEL
(FOUNDED 1733)

The oldest Congregation now practicing Reform Judaism in the United States, Mickve Israel was founded by a group of Jews, mainly of Spanish-Portuguese extraction, which landed at Savannah, July 11, 1733, five months after the establishment of the Colony of Georgia.

The Congregation was incorporated in perpetuity by a special Act of the Georgia Legislature on November 20, 1790. After having worshiped in various temporary quarters for almost a century, in 1820 the Congregation built its own Synagogue – the first in Georgia – at the Northeast corner of Liberty and Whitaker Streets. The present Synagogue was consecrated on April 11, 1878.

In 1789 the Congregation received a letter from President George Washington which stated in part: "May the same wonder-working Deity who long since delivering the Hebrews from their Egyptian oppressors, planted them in the promised land – whose providential agency has lately been conspicuous in establishing these United States as an independent nation – still continue to water them with the dews of Heaven and to make the inhabitants of every denomination participate in the temporal and spiritual blessings of that people whose God is Jehovah."

(Located across from Monterey Square at Bull and Wayne Streets. GHM 025-77, 1961.)

PULASKI MONUMENT

The monument erected in this Square to the memory of General Casimir Pulaski, who fell at Savannah in the cause of American Independence, was completed in 1854. The corner-stone was laid, with impressive ceremonies, October 11, 1853 – the 74th anniversary of the traditional date of the death of the famous Polish patriot.

Dr. Richard D. Arnold was Chairman of the Commissioners in charge of the erection of the memorial for which $20,000 was collected by public subscription.

PULASKI MONUMENT

The designer of the monument, which is of Italian marble, was the eminent Russian-born sculptor, Robert Eberhard Launitz of New York. At the conclusion of his explanation of the elaborate design and its symbolism Mr. Launitz stated:

"The monument is surmounted by a statue of Liberty, embracing with her left arm the banner of the Stars and Stripes, while in her right hand is extended the Laurel Wreath. The love of liberty brought Pulaski to

America; for love of liberty he fought, and for love of liberty he lost his life. Thus, I thought that Liberty should crown his monument, and share with him the homage of the free."

(Located in Monterey Square at Bull and Wayne Streets. GHM 025-23, 1954.)

FORMER HOME
HENRY R. JACKSON
UNION ARMY
HEADQUARTERS, 1865

This building, now the quarters of a private Club, was erected in 1857 for Edmund Molyneux, British consul at Savannah, and served as his residence and as the Consulate until Molyneux's return to England in 1863. In 1865 the Molyneux house was appropriated by the Union army as headquarters for General O.O. Howard and his successor, Gen. Wm. F. Barry. Representatives of the family claimed that furnishings valued at more than $10,000.00 including part of the famous Molyneux wine cellar, were damaged or removed during the Federal occupation.

The mansion was purchased from the Molyneux family in 1885 by Gen. Henry R. Jackson and was the home of that illustrious Georgian until his death in 1898.

Jackson equally distinguished himself as lawyer, soldier, diplomat and poet. He was Judge of the Eastern Circuit of Georgia (1849-'53) and in 1859 was special prosecutor for the United States in the celebrated case of the slave ship "Wanderer." He fought in the Mexican War and won distinction in the Confederate army as a brigadier general. He was ambassador to Austria (1854-'58), and minister to Mexico (1885-'86). A gifted poet, the best known of Jackson's poems is "The Red Old Hills of Georgia."

(Located at Bull and Gaston Streets in front of the Oglethorpe Club. GHM 025-19, 1953.)

GEORGIA
HISTORICAL SOCIETY
FOUNDED 1839

The Georgia Historical Society, founded May 24, 1839, is one of the oldest historical societies in the country. Among its founders were I. K. Tefft, the noted autograph collector; William Bacon Stevens, historian, physician and prelate; and Dr. Richard D. Arnold, who as Mayor of Savannah formally surrendered the City to Gen. Sherman in 1864.

The Presidents of the Society have included John Macpherson Berrien, Attorney General under President Jackson and United States Senator; James M. Wayne, Associate Justice of the Supreme Court of the United States; and Henry R. Jackson, jurist, soldier, diplomat and poet.

Hodgson Hall, the home of the Society, is a repository for books, newspapers and manuscripts relating to the history of Georgia. Dedicated in 1876, the building was a gift of

CARROLL PROCTOR SCRUGGS

HODGSON HALL
HOME OF THE GEORGIA HISTORICAL SOCIETY

Margaret Telfair Hodgson and Mary Telfair as a memorial to William Brown Hodgson, the distinguished scholar of Oriental languages and United States Dragoman and Consul to the Barbary States and Turkey.

(Located at Gaston and Whitaker Streets. GHM 025-13, 1953.)

WARREN A. CANDLER HOSPITAL

Georgia's first hospital, this institution is believed to be the second oldest general hospital in continuous operation in the United States. It was founded in 1803 as a seamen's hospital and poor house and was incorporated in 1808 under the name of Savannah Poor House and Hospital Society. The hospital was removed to this site in 1819.

In 1835 a new charter was obtained for the institution.

During the War Between the States a portion of the Hospital was used

for the care of Confederate soldiers. In the area to the rear a stockade was erected in 1864, around the great oak that still stands there, for confinement of Union prisoners.

After Sherman's occupation of Savannah and until 1866 the building served as a Union hospital.

The name was changed in 1872 to Savannah Hospital. From 1871 to 1888 the Savannah Medical College was located here.

In 1876 the building was completely renovated. However, the structure of the 1819 building was retained and remains as the nucleus of the present hospital.

In 1931 the facilities were acquired by the Methodist Church, and the name changed to honor Bishop Warren A. Candler.

(Located on Huntingdon Street just off Drayton Street at the old entrance to the hospital. GHM 025-84, 1964.) **Note:** You simply *must* see this oak tree. The hospital is still in operation but not at this location.

SAINT PHILLIPS MONUMENTAL A.M.E. CHURCH

The first African Methodist Church in Georgia was organized by the Rev. A.L. Stanford on June 16, 1865, at Savannah, Georgia and was given the name Saint Phillip African Methodist Episcopal Church. Two months and fifteen days later, the Sunday School had its beginning.

Many great preachers have pastored this historic church. One was Bishop Henry M. Turner, a member of the state legislature during Reconstruction and a leader of the Back-to-Africa movement in Georgia, who pastored this church from 1870 to 1874. A storm demolished the church building in September 1896 and the Odd Fellow's Hall was secured for worship until the church could be rebuilt. The General Conference meeting in Waycross in 1897 renamed the church St. Phillips Monumental A.M.E. Church.

Memorial tablets in the church carry the names and dates of service of all the bishops in Georgia and all pastors serving this congregation since the church's beginning.

On May 7, 1961, the Church moved from Hall Street to its present location at Jefferson Street and Park Avenue.

(Located at Jefferson Street and West Park Avenue. GHM 025-91, 1978.)

BIRTHPLACE OF EIGHTH AIR FORCE

On 28 January 1942, the Eighth Air Force was activated in the adjacent building, a National Guard Armory at the time.

Having moved to England, the Eighth was ready on 17 August to test the theory that daylight bombing raids could be made with profitable results. Twelve B-17's participated in this mission, striking the railway marshalling yards at Rouen, France, and returning safely to their home base. This highly successful mission established the pattern for the strategic bombardment of Nazi Germany – the Eighth Air Force by day and the RAF by night.

Under the leaderships of Generals Carl A. Spaatz, Ira C. Eaker and James H. Doolittle, it flew over 600,000 sorties delivering over 700,000 tons of bombs and destroying over 15,000 German aircraft. On one single mission, December 24, 1944, it was able to send 2,000 B-17 Flying Fortresses and B-24 Liberators and nearly 1,000 fighters in the Battle of Germany.

The renowned winged-eight, the emblem of the Eighth Air Force, was designed by former Air Force Major Ed Winter, a native of Savannah.

(Located on Bull Street near Park Avenue in front of the old Chatham Artillery Armory. GHM 025-86, 1966.)

SAILORS' BURIAL GROUND

In this burial ground, hallowed to the "men who go down to the sea in ships and occupy their business in great waters," are interred ship captains and seamen from many lands – America, Norway, Sweden, England, Scotland, Ireland and Germany.

The lot was purchased in 1860 by John Cunningham, a public-spirited citizen of Savannah, as a burial place for seafarers "who may die in this Port." It was presented by Major Cunningham in 1897 to the Savannah Port Society which was incorporated by the Georgia Legislature in 1843 for the purpose of promoting the welfare of "Seamen frequenting the Port of Savannah."

A commemorative service for the officers and men of the merchant marine whose mortal remains lie here is held annually at this site on the Sunday nearest National Maritime Day, May 22nd, which is the anniversary of the departure of the Steamship "Savannah" from this Port on her epoch-making voyage across the Atlantic in 1819.

(Located in Laurel Grove Cemetery North at West 31st Street. GHM 025-17A, 1953.)

JASPER SPRING

On this spot, according to long and persistent tradition, occurred one of Sergeant William Jasper's most famous exploits during the American Revolution. Here, in 1779, at the spring then located along the road to Augusta, Sergeant Jasper and Sergeant John Newton ambushed a detachment of ten British soldiers and liberated several Patriot prisoners who were being taken to Savannah.

While no contemporary confirmation of Jasper's feat exists (it was first publicized by Parson Weems in 1809 in his Life of Gen. Francis Marion), the exploit was in every way characteristic of the immortal sergeant.

An illustration of his courage and resourcefulness is found in the following item published in the VIRGINIA GAZETTE (Williamsburg), May 15, 1779; "The brave serjeant Jasper... has lately given a new proof of his courage and address: He, with another serjeant, a few days ago, crossed the Savannah river, took, and brought to Major General Lincoln's headquarters, two Captains, named Scott and Young, of the British troops in Georgia."

Sergeant Jasper was mortally wounded, Oct. 9, 1779, while heroically bearing the colors of the 2nd South Carolina Continental Regiment in the assault on the British entrenchments at Savannah.

(Located on Augusta Avenue at junction with I-516. GHM 025-48, 1957.)

JASPER SPRINGS 1779

Where Sergeant William Jasper and Sergeant Newton rescued two American prisoners and killed two and captured eight British soldiers in making the rescue.

(Located on Augusta Avenue at Junction with I-516. ACH 025-177, 1930.) ♦ ★ – not standing.

HERMITAGE PLANTATION
1783

Ante bellum plantation home and slave quarters. First railroad in America built and operated here January 1820 and used fifty years in

COURTESY, GEORGIA DEPARTMENT OF ARCHIVES AND HISTORY

COURTESY, GEORGIA DEPARTMENT OF ARCHIVES AND HISTORY

COURTESY, GEORGIA DEPARTMENT OF ARCHIVES AND HISTORY

TOP: HERMITAGE PLANTATION
MIDDLE: HERMITAGE AVENUE OF OAKS
BOTTOM: SLAVE QUARTERS AT HERMITAGE
    PLANTATION

extensive brick (Savannah Gray) making industry.

(Located on Lynes Memorial Parkway near the junction of Bay and Wright Streets. ACH 025-178, 1930.) **Note:** The Hermitage Plantation house was moved to Richmond Hill, GA by Henry Ford in the late 1930's.

THE UNION SIEGE LINE AT THE SAVANNAH AND OGEECHEE CANAL

On Dec. 10, 1864, troops of the Right Wing (15th and 17th Corps) of Gen. Sherman's army (U) moved up the Savannah and Ogeechee Canal from the Dillon's Bridge (Fort Argyle) road (Ga 204) and entrenched along the Dean Forest road facing the Confederate batteries on the north bank of Salt Creek. This point on the canal was within artillery range of the Pine Point battery (C), which restricted daylight travel. From the 12th to the 21st, Leggett's division, 17th Corps (U), held the line from this point on the canal south along the Dean Forest road to the Darien road (US 17).

(Located on Dean Forest Road, 0.7 mile north from junction with US 17/GA 25 South. GHM 025-74, 1959.)

BATTERY JONES

Dec. 1864. Beginning near this point and extending about 500 yards north along the left bank of Salt Creek, astride the old Savannah and Darien (Ogeechee) road, strong earthworks were constructed by Confederate engineers to prevent enemy forces from crossing Salt Creek at Owens' Bridge (on the old road), the only feasible crossing in this area. Designated as "Battery Jones," they were manned by the Terrell (Ga.) Artillery, Capt. John W. Brooks, and mounted 3 32-pdr., 1 20-pdr. and 4 12-pdr., guns.

Its front protected by the marshes and its flanks supported by batteries on its right and left, Battery Jones held Owens' Bridge and the road to Savannah securely against all assaults until the night of Dec. 20th. That night, Savannah was evacuated by the Confederate forces to spare it from a destructive bombardment by heavy siege guns which had been landed at Gen. Sherman's new base at King's Bridge, seven miles south on the Great Ogeechee River, and to prevent the defenders from being trapped in Savannah by the vastly superior Union forces which were closing in on the city. At 8 o'clock, the guns of Battery Jones were rendered useless and its garrison was withdrawn to Savannah and thence across the river into South Carolina.

(Located on US 17/GA 25 South at junction with Dean Forest Road. GHM 025-42., 1957.)

CONFEDERATE DELAYING ACTION

Early in Dec. 1864, Gen. Sherman's army (U) approached Savannah by four routes, the right via Statesboro, the left near the Savannah River. Dec. 6th, Osterhaus' 15th A.C. (U) reached Ogeechee River at Jenk's Bridge (US 80, east of Blitchton). Osterhaus sent Corse's and Smith's divisions down E. bank of the Ogeechee to seize the Savannah and Ogeechee Canal (4 mi. NW), Hazen's and Wood's divisions down W. bank to cross the Canochee River, break the Savannah and Gulf

R. R. at Way's Station (Richmond Hill) and Fleming, then cross the Ogeechee, reassemble the corps in this area, and move on to Savannah.

To delay Osterhaus' advance, Gen. Hardee, CSA, in command at Savannah, sent 600 men and 2 guns to secure this road junction. Earthworks were prepared; the left resting S. of the Old Darien Rd., the right ending north of Dillon's Bridge (Fort Argyle) Road.

Dec. 9th, Corse's div., moved up to attack the position. Adams' brigade, supported by Brunner's battery, deployed astride Dillon's Bridge Rd. Rice's brigade moved to the Darien Rd. to strike the Confederate left. Adams advanced under cover, charged, and forced the outnumbered defenders to retire toward Savannah.

(Located on US 17/GA 25 South at the junction with Canebrake Road near Basin Road. GHM 025-73, 1989).

FORT ARGYLE 1734

Six miles west, site of Fort Argyle, erected 1733 by Oglethorpe. Garrisoned by detachment of rangers. Only important military outpost against Spaniards in 1734.

(Located on US 17/GA 25 South at junction with GA 204. ACH 025-176, 1930.) ♦ ★ – not standing.

OLD INDIAN TRAIL COLONIAL DAYS

This trail was used by Indians in predatory expeditions against South Carolina.

(Located on US 17/GA 25 South at junction with Canebrake Road near Basin Road. ACH 025-175, 1930.)

THE 15TH CORPS AT THE SAVANNAH AND OGEECHEE CANAL

On Dec. 6, 1864, the 15th Corps (U), Maj. Gen. P.J. Osterhaus, USA, the extreme right of Gen. Sherman's army on its destructive March to the Sea, forced a crossing of Great Ogeechee River at Jenk's Bridge (US 80 east of Blitchton) and drove the Confederate defenders toward Savannah. Corse's division crossed and occupied Eden. Smith's division remained on the west bank with the corps trains. With Hazen's and Woods' divisions, Osterhaus moved down the west bank, Hazen to take the bridge over Canoochee River east of Bryan Court House (Clyde),

Woods to prepare crossings over the Ogeechee at Fort Argyle (1 mile W across the river) and on the charred ruins of Dillon's bridge, at the mouth of this canal.

On the 8th, Corse moved down the east bank to this point and found the bridge over the canal in flames. He rebuilt it, then camped here for the night. On the 9th, Smith arrived with the corps trains. Corse moved forward to the Darien road (US 17), defeated a small Confederate force entrenched astride both roads, and drove it toward Savannah. On the 10th, Corse moved north of Little Ogeechee River followed by Hazen who, having secured the bridge over the Canoochee, had crossed the Ogeechee at Dillon's Bridge. Smith moved north along the canal, followed by Woods who had crossed the Ogeechee at Fort Argyle. That night, Corse, Woods and Smith were in line facing the strong Confederate works along Salt Creek, with Hazen in reserve at the Little Ogeechee.

(Located on GA 204 (Fort Argyle Road), 2.4 miles west of junction with I-95. GHM 025-72, 1959.)

KING'S BRIDGE

Dec. 1864. After a 300 mile march which had left a wide belt of destruction from "Atlanta to the Sea," Gen. Sherman's army (U) of about 60,000 men was nearing Savannah. During the first weeks of his campaign, his four widely-spread columns had found adequate supplies on the rich farms and plantations of central and eastern Georgia; but in Chatham

County he found little but rice and rice straw upon which to subsist his men and animals. He needed all classes of supplies, as well as heavy guns with which to conduct a siege. Although a supply fleet, under Adm. Dahlgren, was waiting in nearby anchorages, the ships could not pass Fort McAllister (C) 10 miles downstream at Genesis Point, and all attempts to reduce it by naval bombardment had failed.

On the 13th, Hazen's Div., 15th Corps (U), crossed the river here, moved via "Cross Roads" (Richmond Hill), 2.5 miles south, and Bryan Neck road (Ga 63) to Fort McAllister and overwhelmed it by assault from the rear. The great guns of Fort McAllister silenced, the heavily laden supply ships began to move upstream. A wharf was built here by details from the 17th Corps (U), and King's Bridge became the base from which all supplies, including siege materiel, were distributed to the Union forces.

(Located on US 17/GA 25 at the Ogeechee River. GHM 025-43, 1957.)

WHITE BLUFF
MEETING HOUSE

Here meets the oldest congregation following the Reformed (Calvinistic) theological tradition in continuous service in Georgia. In 1737, 160 Reformed Germans came to Savannah seeking religious freedom. After working their terms as indentured servants the colonists petitioned the Trustees of the colony for a

Reformed minister. In August, 1745 the Trustees acceded to the petition and granted a two-acre tract for the church and a glebe of land for the support of the ministry. The glebe land was officially granted by King George II in 1759. The first minister was John Joakim Zubly who also served in the Second Continental Congress.

(Located on White Bluff Road, 1 mile south of junction with Montgomery Crossroads, in front of the church. GHM 025-92, 1980.)

NICHOLSONBORO

Nicholsonboro Community grew out of the turmoil of the last year of the Civil War and the first years of Reconstruction. General W.T. Sherman's Special Field Order No. 15 reserved the sea islands from Charleston southward, plus abandoned rice fields for thirty miles inland, for freedmen in January 1865. During the next two years the officially appointed agent, but self proclaimed, "Governor" Tunis G. Campbell ruled these lands from his island kingdom on St. Catherines.

When ownership of the lands reverted, 200 former slaves mainly from St. Catherines came here and established their own community in 1868. Ten years later eighteen Negroes signed a mortgage for 200 acres of John Nicholson's land. In four years the thrifty mortgage holders paid the $5,000 and received title in 1882. The community was based upon fishing and farming with Savannah as the primary market. With changes in

NICHOLSONBORO CHURCH

fishing technology and more strin-gent city marketing laws, the eco-nomic base and the community withered. The primary monument to this community is the Nichol-sonboro Baptist Church which had been established with the communi-ty. Two early pastors were Alexander Harris, who served with the Confed-erate Army, and Daniel Wright.

(Located at White Bluff and Old Coffee Bluff Roads, 2.8 miles south of junction with Montgomery Cross-roads. GHM 025-92, 1978.)

CAPTURE OF THE USS "WATER WITCH"

In May, 1864, the USS "Water Witch" (80 officers and men and 4 guns), Lt. Comdr. Austin Pender-grast, USN, was on patrol duty in Ossabaw Sound. On the 31st, Flag-Officer Wm. W. Hunter, CSN, assigned Lt. Thos. P. Pelot, CSN, to command a boat expedition de-signed to surprise and capture the vessel. This expedition – 15 officers and 117 men, in 7 boats – arrived at Beaulieu Battery via Skidway Nar-rows late on June 1st, only to find that "Water Witch" was cruising in St. Catherine's Sound. She returned to Ossabaw Sound next day and anchored for the night in the mouth of Great Ogeechee River, about 1½ miles SSE of Raccoon Key.

About 2 A.M. the 3rd – a dark and stormy night – the boat party ap-proached "Water Witch" in two columns, pulling cautiously with muffled oars. When hailed, Lt. Pelot gave the order to board. The boats closed in, and the boarding parties cut through the nettings and swarmed over the rails. After a desperate fight with cutlass and pis-tol, in which Lt. Pelot – the first aboard – was killed, his men cleared the deck and the ship was theirs.

Lt. Jos. Price, CSN, assumed com-mand. To prevent her recapture, he moved the ship through Hell Gate and up Vernon River to the protec-tion of Beaulieu Battery, whose guns turned back such an attempt on the 5th. At Beaulieu, Lt. W. W. Carnes, CSN, reported on board, assumed command, and moved "Water Witch" up-river to White Bluff to refit her and to receive her new crew.

(From White Bluff Road, take Davidson Avenue east 0.5 mile, continue on Dancy Avenue 0.1 mile to marker. GHM 025-51, 1957.)

GEORGE WHITEFIELD (1714-1770)

BETHESDA:
HIGHLIGHTS OF ITS HISTORY

The interest of George Whitefield in the institution he founded here never flagged. During his lifetime he paid frequent visits to what he called "my beloved Bethesda, surely the most delightful place in all the southern part of America."

Whitefield's will left Bethesda in trust to Selina, Countess of Huntingdon. In 1773 lightning and fire damaged the main building, enlarged 4 years previously by the addition of two wings. Repairs were made as a result of her benevolence.

Her plans to establish a college at Bethesda were thwarted by the American Revolution. During that struggle the Georgia House of Assembly appointed trustees to manage the property.

In 1788, under the patronage of the Countess of Huntingdon, Bethesda was opened as a college. Following her death in 1791 the existing Board of Trustees was incorporated by Act of the Legislature and the State assumed control of the property.

During the next ten years Bethesda fell into decay. Revived in 1801, the school was closed 4 years later following a disastrous fire. In 1855 the Union Society acquired the property and recommenced the great work begun by the Reverend Whitefield.

(Located on Ferguson Avenue off Whitfield Avenue/Diamond Causeway in front of Bethesda. GHM 025-80, 1962.)

BETHESDA: ITS FOUNDING

The idea of establishing an orphanage in Georgia was suggested by Charles Wesley and James Edward Oglethorpe. Enthusiastically embraced by the Reverend George Whitefield, he labored toward that end after his arrival in Georgia in 1738.

Through his efforts substantial sums were raised and a grant of 500 acres obtained in 1739 from the Trustees of the Colony. Site of the Orphan House (far removed from "the wicked influence of the town") was selected by Whitefield's faithful co-worker, James Habersham, who wrote, "The boys and girls will be taught to labor for their souls as well as for their daily bread."

March 25, 1740, Whitefield laid the first brick in the Orphan House to which he gave the name Bethesda, hoping it would ever prove what the word imported, "the House of Mercy." November 3, 1740, 61 children took up residence at the "Great House," described by an English traveler of the period as a "square building of very large dimensions, the foundations of which are of brick, with chimneys of the same; the rest of the superstructure of wood."

Since then hundreds of young people have gone forth from Bethesda's sheltering arms to make their mark in the world, among them Governor John Milledge and General Lachlan McIntosh.

(Located on Ferguson Avenue off Whitfield Avenue/Diamond Causeway in front of Bethesda. GHM 025-81, 1962.)

THE UNION SOCIETY AND BETHESDA

In 1750 the Saint George's Club, a benevolent organization, was founded in Savannah. Of its 5 original members Peter Tondee and Richard Milledge had attended Bethesda. At some time prior to 1765 its name was changed to the Union Society. The organization from its beginning took a deep interest in Bethesda.

The Union Society continued in existence during the American Revolution. While prisoners of the British at Sunbury 4 members of the Society, Mordecai Sheftall, Josiah Powell, John Martin and John Stirk, held a meeting April 23, 1779. The Union Society was incorporated by the Legislature in 1786.

After Bethesda was discontinued in 1805 the Society carried, along with other charitable work, a considerable share of the burden of educating orphan children in the community. In 1854 it purchased 125 acres of the original Orphan House Tract for $2500.00. Buildings were erected and furnished at a cost of $4700.00. The children under the charge of the Society were removed to Bethesda that year.

Past Presidents of Union Society include Mordecai Sheftall, George Houstoun, Noble W. Jones, Joseph Clay, Joseph Habersham, David B. Mitchell, John Macpherson Berrien and Richard D. Arnold.

(Located on Ferguson Avenue off Whitfield Avenue/Diamond Causeway in front of Bethesda. GHM 025-82, 1962.)

SITE OF COLONIAL SHIPYARD

Approximately 300 yards northeast of this marker there was located in colonial days a shipyard where at least one vessel capable of engaging in overseas trade was built. The creek on which it stood is known as Shipyard Creek.

The site of the shipyard was on the Beaulieu (or Bewlie) plantation of John Morel and was favorable for shipbuilding activities because of its accessibility to the Vernon River and the plentiful supply of live oak in the vicinity.

Here, in December, 1774, Daniel Giroud, shipbuilder, constructed the brig "Bewlie," a vessel of 200 tons

burden. In reporting the launching of the ship the "Georgia Gazette" stated that "those who are judges say she is well built and of the best materials, particularly her frame." During the American Revolution Giroud assisted in the construction of several Continental row galleys which saw service in Georgia waters.

(Located on Shipyard Road, 0.4 mile east off Whitfield Avenue. GHM 025-66, 1958.)

MODENA

This location first appears (1734) in Georgia's history as a Savannah outpost. An original settler was Thomas Mouse who is remembered for his description of early hardships here. An evangelical visitor in 1736 was John Wesley. By 1740 the settlement was abandoned.

The Island revived when the Georgia Trusteeship ended in 1753, and Colonial Government established. An early grantee was John Milledge, whose plantation at this site was called "Modena." He was the orphaned son of one of the "First Hundred," the youthful protege of Oglethorpe, Captain of the Rangers, and member of First Commons House of Assembly. His son and successor, John, Jr., was a leader in the American Revolution. He was appointed State Attorney General at the age of 23 when still in uniform, and later became U.S. Representative, Governor and U.S. Senator. As Governor he helped found the University of Georgia (Originally Franklin College). Modena was an active plantation until Mid-Nineteenth Century. The name is thought to come from Modena, Italian seat of silk culture; an industry envisioned for early Georgia, but which did not flourish.

(Located at the Skidaway Institute of Oceanography, Skidaway Island. GHM 025-92, 1981.)

ISLE OF HOPE METHODIST CHURCH

The Isle of Hope Methodist Church was organized in 1851. The first Trustees were George W. Wylly, Simeon F. Murphy, John B. Hogg, William Waite, Theodore Goodwin, Thomas J. Barnsley and the Rev. William S. Baker.

The church building that stands here was erected in 1859 on land given by Dr. Stephen Dupon. Its architecture is similar to that of the early churches at Midway and Ebenezer. The gallery at the rear of the church was built primarily for the accommodations of slaves.

Symbolic of the hospitality extended by the Church to all faiths is the large key that hangs outside the entrance.

During the War Between the States a Confederate battery stood on the church lot, mounting two 8-inch columbiads and two 32-pounder cannon. The church was used as a hospital for Confederates stationed in the area, the pews (still in existence) serving as beds. Thirty-three Effingham County soldiers sleep in the adjoining churchyard.

(Located on Parkersburg Road, Isle of Hope in front of the church. GHM 025-83, 1962.)

SAVANNAH STATE COLLEGE

This state college was established in 1891 as the Georgia Industrial College for Colored Youths as an outgrowth of the Second Morrill Act of 1890 and an Act of the Georgia General Assembly, November 26, 1890, creating this institution as one of the original Negro land-grant colleges.

The initial session was held at the Baxter Street School in Athens from June to August, 1891. In October of the same year, the school sessions began on the present site. Its initial educational program was agricultural, mechanical and literary, and by 1898, the college was able to award its first degree.

It was the first public institution of higher learning to be established for Negroes in the state and now is a part of the University System of Georgia.

The first president (1891-1921) of the college was Major R. R. Wright who, when just a lad, was asked by General O. O. Howard of the Freedman's Bureau what message should he take back to the people of the North. Young Wright's famous answer was, "Just tell them, we are rising." His answer inspired the poet, John Greenleaf Whittier to write the poem, "The Little Black Boy of Atlanta."

(Located off E. Victory Drive, near the Colston Administration building. GHM 025-90, 1978.)

AMERICAN GRAND PRIZE RACES, 1910 AND 1911 VANDERBILT CUP RACE, 1911

On each side of Waters Avenue at this site stood the grandstands built for the famous Savannah automobile races in 1910 and 1911. The starting and finishing line was located in front of the stands.

On November 12, 1910, David Bruce-Brown won the American Grand Prize Race of 415 miles by only one and a half seconds, averaging 70.55 miles an hour in a Benz car. The Grand Prize Race held on November 30, 1911, was also won by Bruce-Brown, driving a Fiat, with an average speed of 74.45 miles per hour.

On November 27, 1911, Ralph Mulford, at the wheel of an American-made Lozier, was victor in the Vanderbilt Cup Race, averaging 74.07 miles an hour.

These races which were run over a course of 17 miles of fine roads in Chatham County are considered by authorities as the greatest automobile road races held in this country. Of international interest and importance, the events contributed their share in the development of the early automobile industry in America.

(Located on Waters Avenue at 46th Street. GHM 025-33, 1955.)

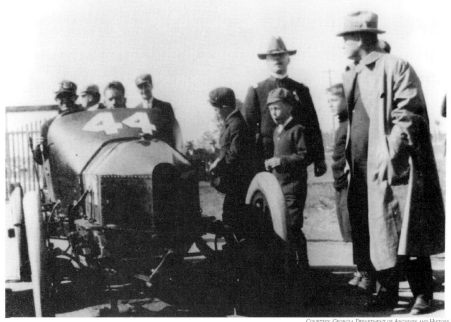

COURTESY, GEORGIA DEPARTMENT OF ARCHIVES AND HISTORY

COURTESY, GEORGIA DEPARTMENT OF ARCHIVES AND HISTORY

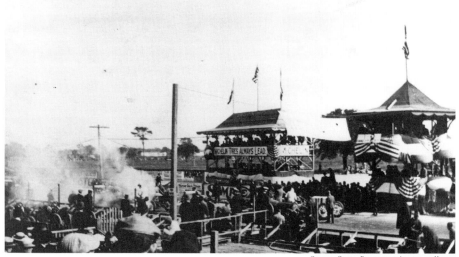

COURTESY, GEORGIA DEPARTMENT OF ARCHIVES AND HISTORY

ABOVE AND PREVIOUS PAGE:

SCENES FROM THE 1910 GRAND PRIZE RACE
HUMOROUS NOTE: *Please notice the sign mounted on the fence post in the top picture.*

TYBEE ISLAND

LAZARETTO

After the repeal of the anti-slavery provision in the Charter of the Colony of Georgia in 1749, an act permitting the importation of slaves ordered the erection of a Lazaretto (Quarantine Station) on Tybee Island. Not until 1767 were 104 acres purchased from Josiah Tattnall for this purpose. Completed the following year, the buildings were situated on the westernmost tip of Tybee, at the mouth of what soon became known as Lazaretto Creek. In its hospital voyagers who arrived ill were treated and those who died were buried in unmarked graves. After continuous use through the Revolution, the Grand Jury reported it in ruinous condition in 1785 and a new station was later erected on Cockspur Island.

(Located on US 80 west of Lazaretto Creek. GHM 025-64, 1958.)

FEDERAL BATTERIES ON TYBEE ISLAND

Between February 21 and April 9, 1862, Federal troops under Gen. Quincy A. Gillmore erected 36 guns in 11 batteries, extending eastwardly on Tybee Island from Lazeretto Creek opposite Fort Pulaski. Two of the Federal batteries consisted of rifled cannon. The work was carried on under cover of darkness and was concealed by day behind a camouflage of branches and brushwood. The Fort was defended by a garrison of 385 men under Col. Charles H. Olmstead of Savannah. Twenty of the 48 guns faced the Federal batteries, but when the bombardment of the fort began from the shore the defenders of the Fort found that they were of insufficient range to damage the attackers. After a continuous bombardment of 30 hours the walls were breached and the Fort was surrendered. It was the first effective use of rifled cannon against a masonry fortification and thus marked an epoch in military history.

(Located on US 80 east of Lazaretto Creek. GHM 025-60, 1958.)

FORT SCREVEN

The Legislature of Georgia in 1786 passed a law providing for a fort on Cockspur or Tybee Island to be named in honor of General James Screven, Revolutionary War hero. It was never built by the state. In 1808 the Federal government obtained jurisdiction over the property on Tybee Island now known as Fort Screven Reservation. Actual title was acquired in 1875 and the post, established in 1898, was in continuous use from the Spanish-American War through both World Wars.

Primarily a Coast Artillery fort, at one time Fort Fremont in South Carolina was under its jurisdiction. It became an Infantry post and finally a school for deep-sea diving. Many distinguished officers saw duty there, including General George C. Marshall as colonel in command. In 1945 Fort Screven was declared surplus by the War Department and acquired by the town of Savannah Beach.

(Located in front of the Tybee Museum at Fort Screven near the lighthouse. GHM 025-58, 1958.)

TYBEE ISLAND

Tybee Island was named by the Indians who came from the interior to hunt and fish. Settled since the beginning of the colony of Georgia, it was the scene in 1775 of the first capture by the first Provincial vessel commissioned by any Congress in America for naval warfare in the Revolution, when a Georgia schooner captured an armed British vessel laden with military stores. In 1776 the royal Governor, Sir James Wright, broke his parol and escaped to a British man of war in Tybee Roads. The Council of Safety ordered all Tybee houses sheltering British officers and Tories destroyed and a raid on the Island by the Patriot forces accomplished this purpose.

In 1779 a large French fleet under Count d'Estaing anchored off Tybee for two months during the siege of Savannah by the French and American forces. In the War Between the States, Federal troops erected batteries here for the reduction of nearby Fort Pulaski. Troops were trained on Tybee Island during both World Wars.

(Located in front of the Tybee Museum at Fort Screven near the lighthouse. GHM 025-62, 1958.)

THE TYBEE LIGHTHOUSE

TYBEE LIGHTHOUSE

A lighthouse on Tybee was one of the first public structures in Georgia. Completed in 1736 by William Blithman of cedar piles and brickwork, its 90 foot height made it the loftiest in America. Destroyed in a storm, it was replaced by another built by Thomas Sumner in 1742 which Oglethorpe called "much the best Building of that kind in America." It was almost entirely rebuilt in 1757 by Cornelius McCarty and James Weyms. In 1773 John Mulryne built the third lighthouse

FORT PULASKI

on a third site. The Mulryne light-house forms the base of the present structure, making part of it of Colonial construction. In 1791 Georgia ceded it with 5 acres to the Federal government. Partially destroyed by the Irish Jasper Greens of Savannah during Union occupation of the island, it was repaired and today is one of the famous lighthouses on the Eastern seaboard.

(Located at the Lighthouse near Fort Screven. GHM 025-59, 1958.)

FORT PULASKI

Named for General Casimir Pulaski, the Polish hero who was mortally wounded at the Siege of Savannah, 1779, Fort Pulaski was built in accordance with plans by General Simon Bernard, formerly chief engineer under Napoleon. Begun in 1829 and completed in 1847, the fort was constructed principally under Lt. J. F. K. Mansfield. There Lt. Robert E. Lee saw his first service after his graduation from West Point.

Pulaski was never garrisoned until its seizure by Georgia troops in January, 1861, to prevent occupation by Federal forces. On April 10, 1862, Federal batteries on Tybee Island commenced the bombardment of Fort Pulaski. After 30 hours of bombardment as a result of which the walls were breached and its guns disabled, Col. Charles H. Olmstead surrendered the Fort. The bombardment marked the first effective use of rifled cannon against a masonry fortification and constituted an epoch in military history.

Abandoned by 1885, Fort Pulaski became a National Monument in 1924 and was placed under the National Park Service in 1933.

(Located on US 80 at the entrance to Fort Pulaski. GHM 025-61, 1958.)

JOHN WESLEY (1703-1791)

On February 6, 1736, John Wesley, the founder of Methodism, landed at Peeper (now Cockspur) Island near here and there preached to his fellow voyagers his first sermon on American soil. A monument has been erected on Cockspur Island to commemorate the event.

Sent to Georgia by the Trustees as missionary, Wesley was the third minister of the Established Church in the colony. He preached in the scattered settlements of Georgia, journeying thither by boat and over Indian trails. Wesley returned to England in 1737 after differences with his parishioners. "I shook off the dust of my feet and left Georgia," he wrote, "having preached the Gospel there (not as I ought, but as I was able) one year and nearly nine months."

(Located at Fort Pulaski near the visitors center. GHM 025-63, 1958.)

THE WAVING GIRL MONUMENT
(Located in downtown Savannah on River Street.)

THE WAVING GIRL

For 44 years, Florence Martus (1868-1943) lived on nearby Elba Island with her brother, the lighthouse keeper, and no ship arrived for Savannah or departed from 1887 to 1931 without her waving a handkerchief by day or a lantern by night. Throughout the years, the vessels in return watched for and saluted this quiet little woman. Few people ever met her yet she became the source of romantic legends when the story of her faithful greetings was told in ports all over the world. After her

COURTESY, GEORGIA DEPARTMENT OF ARCHIVES AND HISTORY

FLORENCE MARTUS (1868-1943)

retirement the Propeller Club of Savannah, in honor of her seventieth birthday, sponsored a celebration on Cockspur Island. A Liberty ship built in Savannah in 1943, was named for her.

(Located at Fort Pulaski near the visitors center. GHM 025-65, 1958.)

GLYNN COUNTY

Named in honor of John Glynn (1722-1779), noted member of Parliament, a friend of the colonies, and who was once Sergeant of London. This was an original county previously organized in 1765 as the parishes of St. David, St. James and St. Patrick. County Seat: Brunswick.

BRUNSWICK

GLYNN COUNTY

Glynn County, one of the eight original Counties of Georgia, was organized under the 1777 Constitution of the State of Georgia. It was named in honor of John Glynn, a member of the British House of Commons who defended the cause of the American Colonies in the difficulties which led to the Revolutionary War.

Glynn County contains the lands formerly included in the Colonial Parishes of St. David, St. Patrick, and St. James, which had been organized in 1758.

Among the early officials were the Hon. George Walton, Signer of the Declaration of Independence, Judge of the Superior Court; James Spalding, Alexander Bissett, Richard

Leake, and Raymond Demere, Justices of the Inferior Court; John Goode, Clerk of the Inferior and Superior Courts; John Palmer, Sheriff; John Burnett, Register of Probates; Richard Bradley, Tax Collector; Martin Palmer, Tax Receiver; Joshua Miller, Surveyor; Jacob Helvestine, Coroner; George Handley (who in 1788 was elected Governor of the State of Georgia) and Christopher Hillary, Legislators; George Purvis, Richard Pritchard, Moses Burnett, John Piles, and John Burnett, Commissioners of Glynn Academy.

(Located at G and Union Streets, on the court house lawn. GHM 063-21, 1957.)

SIDNEY LANIER
GEORGIA'S GREATEST POET

Was a guest in this home on many occasions in the 1870's. It was then the residence of his wife's brother, Henry C. Day.

On these visits Lanier became acquainted with "The Marshes of Glynn" which he immortalized.

(Located on Albany Street just off George Street. GHM 063-2, 1956.)

MARK CARR

Brunswick's first settler came to Georgia in 1738 with Oglethorpe's regiment. He was granted 500 acres at this place, on which he established his plantation.

Several tabby buildings erected by him stood nearby and a military outpost was maintained here.

In 1741 Indians from Florida raided his plantation, causing 750 pounds damage. The Indians killed or wounded some of the soldiers, while others were taken prisoners.

(Located at Union Street and First Avenue. GHM 063-1, 1953.)

LANIER'S OAK

During his visits to Brunswick in the 1870's Sidney Lanier, Georgia's greatest poet, frequently sat beneath this live oak tree and looked out over "a world of marsh that borders a world of sea." Here he received the inspiration which resulted in some of his finest poems. Of these the best known is "THE MARSHES OF GLYNN."

(Located on US 17/GA 25, 0.4 mile south of the road to St. Simons Island. GHM 063-10, 1956.)

LANIER OAK

Beneath this tree Sidney Lanier, a Georgian, composed "The Marshes of Glynn" one of the most admired American Poems.

(Located on US 17/GA 25, 0.4 mile south of the road to St. Simons Island. ACH 063-99, 1930.) ♦ ★ – not standing.

LANIER OAK

BLUE STAR MEMORIAL HIGHWAY

A Tribute to the Armed Forces that have defended the United States of America

Honoring Lt. David Anderson Everett, USN Returned POW from Vietnam.

(Located at the visitor's center on I-95 South between exits 8 and 9. GCG 063-97.)

BOYS ESTATE (ELIZAFIELD PLANTATION) 1/2 MI.

Boys Estate, Georgia's town just for boys, is located one-half mile west of here, on a part of historic Elizafield Plantation. Elizafield, first the home of Dr. Robert Grant, later of his son, Hugh Fraser Grant, was one of the rich River Plantations of the early

19th century. It was cultivated intensively in rice and sugar cane, and the ruins of a large sugar mill built of tabby are still in evidence.

In 1935, Cator Woolford gave this tract to Georgia for a State Park, and in 1945 it was made available by the Legislature for the establishment of Boys Estate.

(Located on US 17/GA 25 North at junction with GA 99. GHM 063-22, 1957.)

HOPETON-ON-THE-ALTAMAHA HOME OF JAMES HAMILTON COUPER 1.4 MI.

Hopeton Plantation, of which Altama is a part, lies about 1.4 miles west of here. A model rice and sugar Plantation of the early 19th century, described in books by several travelers from Europe, Hopeton is best remembered as the home of James

HOPETON-ON-THE-ALTAMAHA
(Painted by John Lord Couper)

JAMES HAMILTON COUPER (1794-1866)

CAROLINE WYLLY COUPER

Hamilton Couper. "A pioneer in the agricultural and industrial development of Georgia and the South," James Hamilton Couper was an archaeologist, a geologist, a conchologist, architect and historian—a man whose abilities and accomplishments would be recognized in any time.

(Located on US 17/GA 25 North at junction with GA 99. GHM 063-23, 1958.)

JEKYLL ISLAND CLUB

JEKYLL ISLAND

JEKYLL ISLAND
9 MI. LONG, 1-1/4 MI. WIDE,
11 MI. OF BEACH.

Jekyll Island , Indian hunting and fishing ground, private stronghold held by Spain for more than a century from 1566, was named by Oglethorpe to honor his friend, Sir Joseph Jekyll, who, with Lady Jekyll, contributed 600 pounds toward the founding of the Colony of Georgia. The great trees on this island are among "Georgia's seven natural wonders." The broad white beach is unexcelled.

Major William Horton, officer of Oglethorpe's Regiment, had his plantation here. Later, Jekyll Island was owned by Clement Martin and by Richard Leake. After the Revolutionary War, the island was owned by Poulain du Bignon and his descendants for a century.

In 1886 , after a world-wide search for a beautiful, healthy, quiet and private vacation site, a group of America's wealthiest men purchased Jekyll Island. For 56 years (1886-1942), members of the exclusive Jekyll Island Club relaxed on the island.

The State of Georgia bought Jekyll Island from the Club in 1947 for a State Park.

(Located on Ben Fortson Parkway at the entrance to the island. GHM 063-14, 1957.) ♦ – removed.

CHARLES SPALDING WYLLY
(A photograph taken in 1905)

tain Alexander Campbell Wylly was born in Belfast in 1759, moving to Savannah from there.

This road is one of the few that now bear names given by the Jekyll Island Club members. What is now Beachview Drive consisted of three shell roads: Morgan (for John Pierpont Morgan); Bourne (for Frederick G. Bourne, Director of Singer Sewing Machine Company and President of Jekyll Island Club 1914-1919); Lanier (for Charles Lanier, original member of Club, and President of Jekyll Island Club 1897-1913). He was a kinsman of Sidney Lanier, poet-author of "Marshes of Glynn."

(Located on Beachview Drive and Captain Wylly Road. GHM 063-29, 1958.)

CAPTAIN WYLLY ROAD

There were two Captain Wyllys in the history of Jekyll. It is believed the road was named for Charles Spalding Wylly (1836-1923). Captain in the Confederate Army, 1st Georgia Regulars, a descendant of Clement Martin, who was granted, on April 5, 1768, Jekyll Island by the Crown. His grandfather, Captain William Campbell Wylly, remaining loyal to the British in the Revolution, took part in the campaign when the British General Prevost crossed the St. Marys and marched on Savannah. After the Revolution he moved to Nassau and was made Governor of New Providence. In 1807 he returned to Georgia, lived first on Jekyll, then St. Simons. Cap-

THE SPANISH ON JEKYLL ISLAND

Within sight and sound of St. Simons Island, Jekyll Island was ideal for entertaining Spanish visitors to the settlement at Frederica. Major William Horton, resident of the island, received the guests while Oglethorpe on St. Simons, with cannon booming and his few soldiers appearing and reappearing on the south beach, professed a strength he did not have.

In 1736, Spanish Commissioners Don Pedro Lamberto and Don Manuel d'Arcy, sent by Governor Sanchez of St. Augustine to discuss rival claims to the Georgia Coast were feted on Jekyll. On board the

Sloop *Hawk* in Jekyll Sound, kilted Highlanders from Darien with clanging broadswords, Tomo-Chi-Chi and Hyllspilli with about 30 of their "chiefest" Indians in war paint and regalia loudly denounced the Spanish and helped Oglethorpe impress the visitors with the strength and good will of the colonists. Agreeing to leave all questions to the courts of Spain and England, the emissaries returned to St. Augustine pleased with their mission. Angered by the decision Spain recalled and executed Governor Sanchez.

After the Battle of Bloody Marsh, the Spaniards burned the buildings on Jekyll Island.

(Located on Beachview Drive at Clam Creek Road. GHM 063-35B, 1959.)

LE SIEUR CHRISTOPHE ANNE POULAIN DU BIGNON (1739-1825) HORTON - DU BIGNON HOUSE DU BIGNON BURIAL GROUND

Beginning with Poulain du Bignon, five du Bignon generations made Jekyll Island one of Georgia's most romantic Golden Isles. This tabby ruin and burial ground alone remain from Jekyll Island's century (1794-1886) as the du Bignon Plantation. Christophe Poulain, native of Lamballe, Brittany, was a much decorated French naval captain whose loyalty to Louis 16th in the French Revolution forced him to flee his patrimonial lands. In 1792 on his ship, the *Sapelo*, he brought his family to the hospitable Georgia Coast.

With four other French royalists, he purchased first Sapelo Island and then Jekyll. By 1794 he acquired Jekyll as his own plantation and enlarged Major Horton's house as his manor. Sea Island Cotton recouped his fortunes and supported a Georgia dynasty of landed aristocracy like that established by his forebears. In 1825 Poulain was buried near du Bignon Creek with a live oak tree as his monument. His son Henri added honors to the island plantation as he made the *Goddess of Liberty* reigning queen of coastal racing boats. And when Henri's grandson, John Eugene du Bignon, sold Jekyll to a group of millionaire capitalists, with them forming the Jekyll Island Club, Poulain du Bignon's island began a new chapter in its fabulous history.

(Located on Riverview and Major Horton Drives. GHM 063-18, 1965.)

POULAIN DU BIGNON AND DU BIGNON BURYING GROUND

This burying ground contains the bodies of several members of the du Bignon family descendants of Le Sieur Christophe Poulain de la Houssaye du Bignon, native of Saint-Malo in Brittany. One of four Frenchmen, former residents of Sapelo Island, who purchased Jekyll Island in 1791, Poulain du Bignon became the sole owner a few years later.

In his youth du Bignon was an officer in the French army in India and served for years fighting against the donimation of Great Britain. Later he commanded a vessel of war sailing under the French flag. He died in 1814 and was buried here near du Bignon Creek with a live oak tree as his only monument.

Sea Island cotton was the principal crop planted on the du Bignon plantation on Jekyll Island and a large acreage was devoted to its cultivation.

The du Bignon family owned Jekyll Island until 1886, when they sold it to a group of millionaires who immediately formed the famous Jekyll Island Club.

(Located on Riverview and Major Horton Drives. GHM 063-18, 1956.) ♦ – not standing.

TABBY

Tabby was the building material for walls, floors, and roofs widely used throughout coastal Georgia during the Military and Plantation Eras. It was composed of equal parts of sand, lime, oyster shell and water mixed into a mortar and poured into forms.

The lime used in tabby was made by burning oyster shell taken from Indian Shell Mounds, the trash piles of the Indians.

The word tabby is African in origin, with an Arabic background, and means "a wall made of earth or masonry." This method of building was brought to America by the Spaniards.

When the Coquina (shell rock) quarries near St. Augustine were opened, hewn stone superseded tabby for wall construction there. Coastal Georgia has no coquina, so tabby continued to be used here even as late as the 1890's.

(Located on Riverview and Major Horton Drives. GHM 063-16, 1956.)

MAJOR WILLIAM HORTON
BORN IN ENGLAND
CAME TO GEORGIA IN 1736
DIED AT SAVANNAH IN 1748

These are the remains of Horton's tabby house. Major Horton, of Oglethorpe's Regiment, the first English resident of Jekyll Island, erected on the north end of Jekyll a two-story dwelling and large barn. He cleared fields here for cultivation of crops which supplied the settlers at Frederica on St. Simons Island, a neighboring island, who would have suffered except for this assistance. Major Horton cut a road across the north end of Jekyll, running east and west, from this tabby house to the beach. This road is still known as the Horton Road.

Major Horton was a trusted officer chosen by James Oglethorpe for important missions. Upon Oglethorpe's final return to England in 1743, Major Horton succeeded him as commander of the military forces of the Colony of Georgia.

Poulain du Bignon, owner of Jekyll Island after the Revolutionary War, repaired the Horton Tabby house

REMAINS OF WILLIAM HORTON'S HOUSE
A fine example of tabby construction

and made it his home. As the du Bignon family grew, wooden wings were added to the house.

(Located on Riverview and Major Horton Drives. GHM 063-15, 1956.)

GEORGIA'S FIRST BREWERY

Large pieces of tabby seen here on the bank of the creek, now known as du Bignon Creek, mark the site and are the remains of the first brewery established in Georgia. Crops of barley, rye and hops, planted and raised in Horton's fields on Jekyll, were used in making beer for the soldiers at nearby Frederica on St. Simons Island.

Major William Horton, of Oglethorpe's Regiment, was the first English

resident of Jekyll Island. The remains of Horton's tabby home stand northeast of this brewery.

(Located on Riverview Drive just south of Major Horton Drive. GHM 063-19, 1956.)

CONFEDERATE BATTERY

In 1861, Confederate battery positions on Jekyll Island were equipped with one 42-pounder gun and four 32-pounder navy guns en barbette, each having about 60 rounds of shot and shell. Casemates, hot shot furnace and magazines are recorded, also. Of greater strength than batteries on St. Simons Island, the earthworks of palmetto logs, heavy timber, sandbags, and railroad irons were mounted for the protection of Brunswick.

February 10, 1862, Gen. Robert E. Lee requested permission from Gov. Joseph E. Brown to dismantle the stronghold as "the inhabitants of the island and Brunswick have removed themselves and property" to inland points. Maj. Edward C. Anderson removed the guns, sending them to Savannah.

March 9, 1862, Lt. Miller of the USS Mohican landed a rifle company and marines, hoisting the Union flag over the island.

In January, 1863, to strengthen fortifications at Port Royal, S. C., a Federal force was sent by flatboat to seize the railroad irons. Some of the men who had helped build the defenses guided the detachment to them and "the men enjoyed demolishing them far more than they had relished their construction."

(Located on Riverview Drive south of the Horton house, next to the airport. GHM 063-38, 1959.)

BROWN COTTAGE CHIMNEY
McEvers Bayard Brown
New York Banker

This chimney is all that remains of the cottage of Bayard Brown, original member of Jekyll Island Club. In his gay, young days, he built this cottage at Jekyll, overlooking the marshes. He erected a bridge to reach the isolated house, built stables for his horses, and furnished the cottage elegantly for his bride-to-be. But the wedding never came off. The house deteriorated and was torn down.

This eccentric millionaire was known as "The Hermit of the Essex Coast" in England. At the age of 37, he became an exile from America, sailing on his yacht Valfreyia. "Unrequited love" is said to be the cause of his renouncing his native land to become a legendary port-bound yachtsman for 36 years. On the Essex Coast, his yacht engines were always in readiness for a sea voyage. His crew of 18 waited in vain for the order to put to sea.

One thing was certain, Mr. Brown had plenty of money—a million dollars a year, according to one account. Sometimes he would toss gold sovereigns from his yacht for anyone to pick up. Anyone who mentioned "America" in his presence was dismissed.

He died in 1926 requesting that his body be returned to America on the Valfreyia.

(Located on Riverview Drive, at the south edge of the airport. GHM 063-27, 1958.)

JENNINGS COTTAGE
"VILLA OSPO"

This cottage was erected in 1928 by Walter Jennings, capitalist of New York. It has a total of twenty rooms, including ten bedrooms, five baths, and coach house. A feature of the spacious cottage is the 24 x 40 foot paneled living room and the arched hallway leading to it. It also has a large patio with a lily pool and fountain.

"VILLA OSPO"

"SOLTERRA"

Mr. Jennings, was President of the Jekyll Island Club from 1927 to 1933. He was born in San Francisco on September 14, 1858, and died at his winter cottage at Jekyll January 9, 1933. His sisters, Mrs. Gordon Auchincloss, Mrs. Walter Belknap James, and Miss Annie Jennings, were also members of the Club.

Mr. Jennings was one of the first Directors of the Standard Oil Company of New Jersey and Secretary from 1908-1911; Trustee of the New York Trust Company; President, National Gas Company; Director, Bank of Manhattan. He was married in 1891 to Jane Pollock Brown. They had three children, Oliver Burr, Jeanette, and Constance.

He was a member of the University Club, Metropolitan Club of New York, and owned a stock farm in Long Island.

(Located on Riverview Drive north of the hotel. GHM 063-25, 1958.) ♦ – removed.

CRANE COTTAGE; SOLTERRA

Crane Cottage (20 rooms; 17 baths) was built in 1916 by Richard Crane of Crane Company at a cost of $500,000.00. Solterra, the island home of Frederick Baker, New York banker, was on the site until it burned in 1910. On March 20, 1899, President and Mrs. William McKinley and the President's mentor, Senator Mark Hanna of Ohio, were guests at Solterra. Veiled in secrecy, their visit to Jekyll Island was made to plan McKinley's political future. At Solterra Andrew Carnegie was honored at an elaborate banquet. Among the guests were Joseph Pulitzer, J. P. Morgan, the elder, William Rockefeller, George F. Baker.

(Located on Riverview Drive north of the hotel. GHM 063-37, 1959.) ♦ – removed.

GOULD CASINO

This auditorium was the Gould Casino during the Jekyll Island Club Era (1886-1942). It was built by Edwin Gould, son of Jay Gould, who lived at Chichota Cottage.

This playhouse contained, on the first floor, an indoor tennis court, lockers and restrooms, a bowling alley, rifle range, a bedroom. On the second floor were spacious well furnished club rooms. Attached to the casino was a conservatory and a separate garden house.

(Located on Plantation Road north of the hotel at the auditorium. GHM 063-26, 1958.) ◆ – removed.

SHRADY-JAMES COTTAGE
"CHEROKEE COTTAGE"

This cottage has a total of 20 rooms, plus 8 baths. There are 12 bedrooms, 2 kitchens (one for the servants), and a service elevator. It was erected around 1915 for Mrs. Hester E. Cantine Shrady, widow of Dr. George Frederick Shrady of New York (born 1837—died 1907). An eminent physician, Dr. Shrady was editor of the Medical Record, and Assistant Surgeon, U.S.A., during the War Between the States. He attended ex-President U.S. Grant, as consulting surgeon, in his last illness. Mrs. Shrady was the mother-in-law of Edwin Gould, a Jekyll Island Club member. Mr. Gould, who owned the cottage "Solterra" on Jekyll, was the son of the famous financier Jay Gould, who left an estate of over $60,000,000.

The cottage was last occupied by Dr. Walter Belknap James of New York (born in Baltimore 1858— died 1927). He was president of The Jekyll Island Club 1919-1927. He married Helen Goodsell Jennings, sister of Walter Jennings, also a pres-

"CHEROKEE COTTAGE"

ident of Jekyll Island Club. Dr. James was a graduate of Yale, Johns Hopkins, and did graduate work in Germany and Austria. He was consulting physician, Bellevue Hospital, New York, and president of the national committee for Mental Hygiene.

The swimming pool in front of the former Club House was dedicated "in loving memory" to Dr. James by the Jekyll Island Club.

(Located on Plantation Road behind the hotel. GHM 063-24, 1958.) ◆ – removed.

JEKYLL ISLAND CLUB WHARF

Here anchored the most luxurious pleasure craft in the world during the existence of the Jekyll Island Club, 1886-1942.

No other yacht was comparable to John Pierpont Morgan's several *Corsairs*. *Corsair II*, too large to dock, anchored in the channel. Morgan was escorted ashore by a flotilla of small craft, after a cannon had sounded off his arrival in these waters. *Corsair II* was 304 ft. overall, beam 33½ ft., draft 17 ft., speed 19 knots, tonnage 1,600. About this *Corsair*, Morgan, when asked how much it cost, made his classic remark: "If you have to consider the cost you have no business with a yacht."

Other palatial yachts owned by Jekyll Island Club members were: Pierre Lorillard's *Caimen*, James Stillman's *Wanda*, Astor's *Nourmahal*, Vanderbilt's *Alvah* and *Valiant*, H. Manville's *Hi Esmaro, Jr.*, Pulitzer's *Liberty*, George F. Baker's *Viking*, E.T. Stotesbury's *Castle*, Crane's *Illyria*, Theodore N. Vail's *Speedwell* and *Northwind*, Commodore Frederick Bourne's *Marjorie*, Gould's *Hildegards*, *Saono*, and *Ketchum*. Edwin Gould built a private dock in front of his cottage, "Chichota." Andrew Carnegie, whose family owned Cumberland Island, visited Jekyll on yachts, *Skibo* and *Missoe*.

(Located off Riverview Drive at the Wharf. GHM 063-28, 1958.)

MESS KETTLE FROM THE "WANDERER"

This mess kettle from the slave yacht, WANDERER, was used for feeding the slaves landed on Jekyll Island in 1858 – the last slaves brought from Africa to the United States.

The WANDERER, pleasure yacht, slave ship, gunboat, and coastal freighter, was launched in 1857, built by Joseph Rowland and Thomas Hawkins at East Setauket, Long Island, for J. D. Johnson, a wealthy Louisiana planter and mem-

THE YACHT "WANDERER"

ber of the exclusive New York Yacht Club. Sold almost immediately to Johnson's protege W.C. Corrie of Charleston, the WANDERER was used in the illicit slave trade by Corrie and his associates, Charles A. L. Lamar of Savannah and Nelson C. Trowbridge of New Orleans.

At the outbreak of war in 1861, the WANDERER was caught in southern waters by the blockade and seized by Federal forces whereupon she was pressed into Union service in the Pensacola area. After the war she was sold at auction and put into the West Indian fruit trade. The WANDERER was finally driven ashore and wrecked in 1871 on Cape Maisi, Cuba.

(Located off Riverview Drive at the Wharf. GHM 063-17, 1962.) ♦ – removed.

MORGAN TENNIS COURT

Tennis, golf, bowling, croquet, polo, and skeet were the active sports during the existence of the Jekyll Island Club. "Bowling on the green" and croquet were played on the Club

House lawn. The skeet and polo fields were located beyond the Jennings Cottage. The Club's facilities for tennis were exceptional. In addition to the three outdoor courts of native clay, there were two indoor courts, the John Pierpont Morgan and the Edwin Gould Tennis Courts. The Club maintained a tennis pro who was, for many years, Frank Bonneau.

This was the scene of many important tournaments. As a prime sport, tennis was established in 1911 when Richard Crane placed his cup for a mixed doubles handicap. This tournament was played during March. The Annual Invitation Men's Doubles Round Robin was established in 1936, with a cup offered each year by Alanson B. Houghton, former Ambassador to London and Berlin. Winners of the trophy include Bernon S. Prentice, Alexander Thayer, G. Peabody Gardner, H. R. Guild, George A. Lyon, Amory L. Houghton, Cranston Holman, Julian S. Myrick, Watson Washburn, Robert P. Brown, Jr.

(Located on Plantation Road behind the hotel. GHM 063-32, 1958.) ♦ – removed.

SANS SOUCI; CLUB COTTAGE

Known as the J.P. Morgan Cottage because the Morgans, elder and younger, lived here, Sans Souci (Without Care), containing six apartments, was built in 1899 by a corporation of members of the Jekyll Island Club. Among the members who stayed here were: James J. Hill,

"SANS SOUCI"

St. Paul, Minnesota, president of the Great Northern System; Frederick G. Bourne, capitalist; Pierre Lorillard, Tuxedo Park, N.Y., tobacco magnate; J. A. Scrymser, New York, cable and telegraph promoter and a partner of J. P. Morgan in various enterprises; Robert G. Pyne, New York banker.

During the War Between the States the DuBignon family, fearing Union raids, left Jekyll Island, moving inland. After the war, John Eugene DuBignon returned to find his fields devastated and buildings destroyed. The plantation economy never recovered from the ravages and changes made by the war. In the early 1880's, DuBignon built his residence where Sans Souci now stands. In 1886 he sold the island to the Jekyll Island Club for $125,000.00 and became one of the original members. His home was known as the Club Cottage.

(Located just south of the hotel. GHM 063-36, 1959.) ♦ – removed.

COURTESY, AT&T ARCHIVES

THEODORE N. VAIL (1845-1920)

FIRST TRANSCONTINENTAL CALL

Theodore N. Vail, New York, President of the American Telephone and Telegraph Company, participated in a memorable telephone ceremony, January 15, 1915 – January 25, 1915, while recuperating from lameness at Jekyll Island. In order that President Vail might participate in the long circuit call from Jekyll to Washington, New York, and San Francisco. a thousand miles of cable were run to the Island.

Dr. Alexander Graham Bell was the chief figure in the New York call with Thomas A. Watson, assistant to Dr. Bell, at the San Francisco terminal. President Woodrow Wilson, in speaking to Mr. Vail at Jekyll, said, "Hello, Mr. Vail!" "Who is this?" (Mr. Vail). "This is the President. I have just been speaking across the continent." "Oh, yes." (Mr. Vail). "Before I give up

the telephone, I want to extend my congratulations to you on the consummation of this remarkable work," replied the President of the United States. It has been said that Bell created the telephone and Vail created the telephone business.

Mr. Vail visited Jekyll in two yachts at various seasons, *The Speedwell* and *The Northwind.*

(Located on Riverview Drive south of the hotel near Indian Mound. GHM 063-30, 1958.) ♦ – removed.

"INDIAN MOUND" ROCKEFELLER COTTAGE

This cottage was built by the younger brother of John D. Rockefeller, William G. Rockefeller (1841-1922), one of the millionaire members of the Jekyll Island Club. Built about 1900, it was called "Indian Mound" because of its adjacency to the old Indian Mound, believed to be a burial mound of the Guale Indians, of Muskhogean stock, who were the earliest inhabitants of Jekyll Island.

(Located on Riverview Drive south of the hotel. GHM 063-20, 1958.) ♦ ★ – removed.

CLAFLIN-PORTER COTTAGE "MISTLETOE"

The first resident of Mistletoe Cottage (15 rooms; 5 baths) was John Claflin, trustee of many financial and charitable corporations and Brooklyn merchant. He was negoti-

ROCKEFELLER COTTAGE – "INDIAN MOUND"

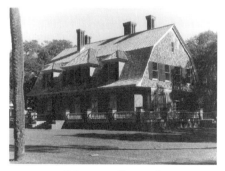

"MISTLETOE COTTAGE"

ating with John Eugene duBignon to purchase Jekyll Island for himself when it was purchased by the Jekyll Island Club. He became an original member.

Henry Kirke Porter, Pittsburgh manufacturer of light locomotives, was elected a member of the Jekyll Island Club in 1891. He was a Member of Congress, 31st Pennsylvania District, 1903-1905.

(Located on Riverview Drive south of the hotel. GHM 063-33, 1959.)
♦ – removed.

PULITZER-ALBRIGHT COTTAGE

On this site was the cottage of Joseph Pulitzer, editor of the St. Louis *Post Dispatch* and New York *World*. His bequests established the School (now Graduate School) of Journalism at Columbia University and the Pulitzer Prize program.

After Pulitzer's death, his 26-room island residence, built in 1903, was purchased by John Joseph Albright, art patron and coal magnate of Buffalo, New York. Among the distinguished guests of the Albrights on Jekyll Island was the English poet, Alfred Noyes.

Servants lived in a 12-room separate cottage. This building was bought by Frank L. Goodyear and moved to its present location. He gave it to the Jekyll Island Club as an infirmary and renamed it Goodyear Memorial Infirmary in memory of his mother, Mrs. Josephine L. Goodyear. From January to April, the infirmary was staffed each season by doctors from Johns Hopkins Hospital in Baltimore.

(Located on Riverview Drive south of the hotel. GHM 063-34B, 1959.)
♦ – removed.

M. E. THOMPSON AND THE PURCHASE OF JEKYLL ISLAND

Melvin E. Thompson, Acting Governor, 1947-1949, was born in Millen, Jenkins County, Georgia, in 1903. After a career as educator and public servant, Thompson was elected Lieutenant Governor for the term beginning January, 1947. following the death of Governor-Elect Eugene Talmadge, shortly before his inauguration, Thompson became Acting Governor until the next scheduled general election.

During his term as Acting Governor, one of his contributions to the state was the acquiring of Jekyll Island for $675,000. The state acquired Jekyll Island by a court condemnation decree, a bargain which has been compared to the original purchase of Manhattan Island. Jekyll Ilsand has proved to be one of Georgia's greatest assets as a year round resort area.

(Located near the junction of Riverview Drive and Stable Road south of the hotel. JI/SPA 063-96, 1963.)

THE BOAT HOUSE SITE

This is the site of the Jekyll Island Club Boat House where the 100-foot steamer *The Jekyll Island* was stored during the off season. (The Club season was usually from after New Year's until before Easter.)

There was no Jekyll Creek bridge (dedicated 1954), no Sidney Lanier bridge (opened 1956) in the Jekyll Island Club Era. Many Club members entrained to Brunswick on their plush private railroad cars. There they were met at the wharf by the steamers *The Jekyll Island*; *The Hattie*; *The Sybil* (45 foot Naphtha Launch named for Sybil Brewster); *The Kitty* (named for Kitty Lawrence, niece of Charles Lanier, a President of the Club). These launches were used as pleasure craft at the convenience of the Club members for fishing, excursions, and to bring supplies and mail from Brunswick.

Other members arrived by yacht at the dock or, if the craft was too large for the shallow water there, anchored in the channel and were brought to shore by smaller craft.

James A. Clark was Captain of Boats and summer manager of the Jekyll Island Club for over forty years.

(Located off Riverview Drive south of the Wharf. GHM 063-31, 1958.)

ST. SIMONS ISLAND

GASCOIGNE BLUFF

Throughout the ages Gascoigne Bluff has been the gateway to St. Simons Island. An Indian village was located here. Capt. James Gascoigne of HM Sloop-of-war HAWK, which convoyed the Frederica settlers on their voyage across the Atlantic in 1736, established headquarters for Georgia's naval forces and had his plantation here. In the Invasion of 1742 the Spaniards landed at this Bluff.

Live oak timbers for the building of USS CONSTITUTION, better known as "OLD IRONSIDES," and the other vessels of our first US Navy were cut on St. Simons and loaded here in 1794 for shipment North where the vessels were built.

During the Plantation Era these lands became the sea island cotton plantation of James Hamilton. A wharf here was the shipping center for the St. Simons plantation.

1874-1902 this Bluff was lined with great mills, where cypress and long-leaf yellow pine timbers were sawed into lumber and shipped to all parts of the world.

The causeway built in 1924, connecting St. Simons with the mainland, has its terminus here.

In 1949 the Methodist Church acquired the upper part of the Bluff and established EPWORTH-BY-THE-SEA as a Conference Center.

(Located in small park upon entering St. Simons Island from the causeway, GHM 063-13, 1956.) **Note:** An identical marker may be found at the junction of Hamilton Road and Arthur J. Moore Drive. Upon entering the island bear left for 0.3 mile, turn left on New Sea Island Road and follow for 0.1 mile, turn left on Hamilton Road and follow for 0.2 mile. GHM 063-12, 1956.

DEMERE ROAD

From the site of the Battle of Bloody Marsh to the intersection with Ocean Boulevard, this road is part of the Military Road, sometimes called the King's High Road, which was built by Frderica settlers in 1738 to connect Fort Frederica and Fort St. Simons. It was used by British and Spanish forces during the Spanish invasion of 1742 and is the only part of the old Military Road still in use.

(Located at Demere Road and East Beach Causeway. GHM 063-3, 1989.)

OLD SPANISH GARDEN

Spain maintained missions along this coast for more than a century. Beginning in 1568 Jesuit and, later, Franciscan missionaries labored to Christianize the Indians and cultivated in the mission gardens figs, peaches, oranges and other plants introduced from Europe. Due to Indian uprisings, pirate raids and British depredations these missions were removed further south in 1686.

A map of St. Simons Island made in 1739 by Capt. John Thomas, engineer in Oglethorpe's Regiment, locates an "OLD SPANISH GARDEN" near this site. In this area materials from the Spanish mission period have been found.

(Located at Demere Road and Ocean Boulevard. GHM 063-6, 1954.)

DELEGAL'S FORT

The first fortification built by the British on the South End of St. Simons Island was erected near this site in April, 1736, by soldiers of the South Carolina Independent Company under command of Lieutenant Philip Delegal. Before coming to St. Simons these soldiers had been stationed at Fort Frederick, near Port Royal, South Carolina.

The fortification erected here, known as "Delegal's Fort at Sea Point," commanded the entrance to the harbor, being located "so that all ships ... must pass within shot of the point."

In 1738, when a regiment of British soldiers was brought to St. Simons Island, Lieutenant Delegal and his soldiers were taken into Oglethorpe's Regiment. Fort St. Simons was then built, taking the site of Delegal's Fort. Most of the area covered by this fortification has been washed away.

(Located on Ocean Boulevard, 0.1 mile north of junction with Demere Road. GHM 063-39, 1961.)

SLAVE CABIN

This tabby slave cabin of Retreat Plantation, now the Sea Island Golf Course, was one of eight cabins that stood in this area, known as New Field. The slaves who lived here tilled the Sea Island cotton fields nearby.

Each of these cabins was 48 x 18 ft. with a partition and a chimney in the center. They stood about 300 feet apart and were shaded by beautiful live oak trees.

Retreat Plantation, originally the property of the Spalding family, was sold to Major William Page whose daughter, Anna Matilda Page, married Hon. Thomas Butler King, M.C.

(Located at Frederica and Demere Roads. GHM 063-7, 1954.)

HARRINGTON HALL

Capt. Raymond Demere, a native of France, served many years in the British army at Gibraltar before coming to Georgia in 1738 as an officer in Oglethorpe's Regiment. His home, Harrington Hall was located at this site.

Later generations of the Demere family lived at the south end of St. Simons Island where their plantation was called Mulberry Grove.

(Located on Lawrence Road, 0.6 mile past junction with Frederica Road. GHM 063-9, 1954.)

GERMAN VILLAGE

Here in 1736, Oglethorpe settled a group of German Lutherans, known as Salzburgers, and their settlement was called the German Village. These Salzburgers made their living by planting, fishing, and selling their products to the Frederica settlers. When Oglethorpe's regiment was disbanded in 1749 the Salzburgers left St. Simons Island.

During the Plantation Era, the Wylly family lived here, their plantation being called "The Village."

(Located on Lawrence Road at Village Drive, 1.2 miles past junction with Frederica Road. GHM 063-8, 1954.)

SINCLAIR PLANTATION

This was the plantation of Archibald Sinclair, tything man of the town of Frederica. In 1765 it was granted to Donald Forbes as bounty land for his services in Oglethorpe's regiment. Forbes sold to Gen. Lachlan McIntosh of Revolutionary fame, whose son, Major William McIntosh, lived and died in the old plantation house. Here, in the family burial plot, lie the bodies of Major McIntosh and his two children. The Agricultural and Sporting Club of St. Simons Island, an organization of plantation owners founded in 1832, used the old tabby home as their club house.

(Located on Lawrence Road, 1.8 miles past junction with Frederica Road. GHM 063-4A, 1954.)

MILITARY ROAD

This Military Road, built in 1738, connected Fort Frederica and Fort St. Simons.

Near this point the road passed the tabby cottage where General Oglethorpe established the only home he had in America. This cottage, shaded by great live oak trees, was surrounded by a garden and an orchard of oranges, figs and grapes.

During the Spanish invasion of Georgia in 1742 a battle was fought here. On the morning of July 7th approximately two hundred Spanish soldiers reached this place, where they were met by Oglethorpe with four platoons of his regiment and the Highland Independent Company from Darien. In this engagement the Spaniards were routed, "upwards of 100" being killed and sixteen taken prisoner. Oglethorpe took two prisoners with his own hands.

The Spaniards, pursued by the British, retreated to their camp at the south end of St. Simons. In the afternoon of the same day, at a place five miles south and on this same road, another battle, known as the Battle of Bloody Marsh, was fought. This, too, was a British victory, ending the threat of Spanish domination of Georgia.

(Located on Frederica Road, 0.4 mile south of Christ Episcopal Church. GHM 063-40, 1984.) ◆

THE SHELL ROAD TO FREDERICA, "THE MILITARY ROAD"

CHRIST CHURCH CEMETERY

Here are buried former Rectors of Christ Church and their families, the families of early settlers and of plantation days, officers of the British Army, and soldiers of every war in which our country fought. The oldest tombstone is dated 1803 but it is believed that there were a number of burials here before that time.

(Located on Frederica Road at Christ Episcopal Church. GHM 063-35A, 1958.)

THE WESLEY OAK

Not far from this spot stood the "great tree" under which Charles Wesley had prayers and preached, March 14, 1736, the first Sunday after his arrival. There were about twenty people present, among whom was Mr. Oglethorpe.

A year later, George Whitfield, appointed by the Bishop of London to serve as Deacon at Savannah and Frederica, wrote in his Journal (August 8, 1737): "In the evening we had publick Prayers, and expounding of the second Lesson under a large tree, and many more present than could be expected."

A wooden Cross made from a tree long designated as the Wesley Oak hangs on the wall of Christ Church near the pulpit.

(Located on Frederica Road at Christ Episcopal Church. GHM 063-34A, 1958.)

CHRIST EPISCOPAL CHURCH

CHRIST EPISCOPAL CHURCH

This congregation was established as a mission of the Church of England in February, 1736. The Rev. Charles Wesley, ordained priest of that Church, conducted the first services in the chapel within the walls of Fort Frederica. The Rev. John Wesley, Rector of Christ Episcopal Church, Savannah, also served this mission. Under the name of St. James, this was one of the eight original parishes established in 1758. After the Revolution, this and other churches which had been served continuously by clergymen of the Church of England formed the Protestant Episcopal Church in the United States of America. Christ Church was incorporated by the State Legislature in 1808 and given a glebe of 108 acres; and in 1823 was one of the three parishes organizing the diocese of Georgia. The first church built on this property in 1820 was almost destroyed during the War Between the States. The present building was erected on the same site in 1884.

(Located on Frederica Road at Christ Episcopal Church. GHM 063-33A, 1958.)

WILLIAM BARTRAM TRAIL TRACED 1773-1777

In 1774 William Bartram came to Frederica. He explored St. Simons Island and noted the flora and beautiful live oaks.

(Located on Frederica Road near the entrance to Fort Frederica National Monument. BTC/GCG 063-95, 1990.)

THALMANN

OLD POST ROAD

This road, formerly an Indian trail which parallelled the coast, was used by the Spanish and British. In 1778 it was traveled by Revolutionary soldiers who marched against Fort Tonyn. The first mail service south of Savannah was established over this road in 1763. Later it became a regular stage coach route. At Coleridge, a short distance north of the present Waycross Highway, Job Tyson maintained a tavern for travelers along the post road. It was the only hostel between the Altamaha and Satilla rivers and was a regular stage coach stop.

(Located on GA 32, 2.9 miles west of Thalmann near the Brantley County line. GHM 063-4B, 1956.)
♦ ★

LIBERTY COUNTY

Named "Liberty" in recognition of the marked patriotism of the Midway community during the Revolutionary War, and in honor of American Independence. This was an original county, previously organized in 1758 as the parishes of St. John, St. Andrew and St. James. County Seat: Hinesville.

FLEMINGTON

OLD SUNBURY ROAD

This route is the Old Sunbury Road, one of the longest vehicular thoroughfares of post-Revolutionary Georgia. It was laid out in the early 1790's from Greensboro via Sparta and Swainsboro to the port of Sunbury on the Midway River. The long way was noted for its elevated course and small number of stream crossings. When Sunbury, which was once Georgia's second port, declined in commercial importance the road lost arterial significance. Many stretches of the old route, however, continue in daily use.

(Located on US 84/GA 38 at the junction of Oglethorpe Boulevard and Old Sunbury Road. GHM 089-7, 1956.)

FLEMINGTON PRESBYTERIAN CHURCH

Organized in 1815 as the Church and Society of Gravel Hill, this was a branch of Midway Church. The Rev. Robert Quarterman was the first pastor. The first edifice was built in 1836 on land donated by Simon Fraser. This one was completed in 1852. Named Flemington in 1850 honoring William Fleming, it was separated from Midway in 1865. In 1866 it was admitted to the Georgia Presbytery with the Rev. D.B. Buttolph, pastor; W.E.W. Quarterman, Thomas Cassels, Ezra Stacy, James Laing, elders; S.A. Fraser, L.M. Cassels, deacons. Ezra Stacy was first Sunday School Super-

FLEMINGTON PRESBYTERIAN CHURCH

intendent. Bell and silver communion service are from Midway Church.

(Located on the Old Sunbury Road, 0.8 mile from Oglethorpe Boulevard/US 84/GA 38. GHM 089-10, 1957.)

HINESVILLE

LIBERTY COUNTY

Liberty County, an original county, was created by the Constitution of Feb. 5, 1777 from Creek Cession of May 20, 1733. It had been organized in 1758 as the Parishes of St. John, St. Andrew and St. James. The theatre of many important events during the Revolution, Liberty County was named for American Independence. From it all of Long and McIntosh Counties were formed. Samuel Morecock was commissioned Sheriff in 1778. Wm. Barnard became Surveyor, Feb. 17, 1782. Francis Coddington in 1785 was made Clerk of

Inf. and Sup. Courts of Liberty, Glynn and Camden Counties. John Lawson was sworn in as Coroner in 1790.

(Located at Commerce and Midway Streets on the court house lawn. GHM 089-6, 1956.)

FORT MORRIS CANNON

This small cannon was a part of the armament of historic Fort Morris at Sunbury during the American Revolution. In November, 1778, a superior British force from Florida under Colonel Fuser of the 60th Regiment besieged the Fort. To the ultimatum to surrender the American Commander, Colonel John McIntosh, sent back the laconic reply: "COME AND TAKE IT." The enemy thereupon abandoned the siege and retired southward.

In January, 1779, the British returned to Sunbury by water. Fort Morris was then under the command of Major Joseph Lane of the Continental army. Ordered by his superiors to evacuate Sunbury following the fall of Savannah, Lane found reasons to disobey and undertook to defend the post against the overwhelming British force under General Augustin Prevost. After a short but heavy bombardment the Fort surrendered on January 9, 1779, with its garrison of 159 Continentals and 45 militia.

This cannon, which was excavated at the site of the ruins of the famous Revolutionary fortification

FORT MORRIS CANNON

in 1940, stands here as a reminder of America's hard-won struggle to achieve Independence.

(Located at Main and Midway Streets, on the court house lawn. GHM 089-22, 1958.)

LIBERTY ARMORY SITE

Returning from the Revolution, the soldiers of Liberty County re-organized themselves into a troop of cavalry, known as the Liberty Dragoons, later the Liberty Independent Troop, the oldest cavalry company in Georgia. In continuous existence since that time, this military company has participated in every war in which this country has been engaged since the Revolution. As late as 1916 the troop served as a cavalry company on the Mexican Border.

When the company went to France in World War I, it was converted to Company B, 106th Field Signal Battalion. In World War II, it became Battery B, 101st Anti-Aircraft Artillery Gun Battalion and took part in the campaign in New Guinea. Dur-

ing the Korean conflict the battery served at Camp Stewart, Ga., and at Camp McCoy, Wisconsin.

At this armory site have taken place some of the most brilliant and colorful tournaments and parades of the Old South.

(Located on US 84/GA 38 at 101st Coast Artillery Drive. GHM 089-4A, 1954.)

SKIRMISH AT HINESVILLE

On Dec. 16, 1864, a detachment of the 7th Illinois Infantry (mounted), foraging near the right flank of Gen. Sherman's army (U) which was then closing in on Savannah, met here in Hinesville a detachment of cavalry from Brig. Gen. Alfred Iverson's brigade of Maj. Gen. Joseph Wheeler's cavalry corps of the Army of Tennessee (C). Wheeler's corps and units of the Georgia Militia had offered steady resistance to Gen. Sherman's "March to the Sea" from Atlanta to Savannah. After a sharp skirmish through the town, the Confederate detachment withdrew toward the Canoochee River to rejoin Iverson.

(Located on US 84/GA 38/Oglethorpe Avenue, near junction with GA 196. GHM 089-24, 1958.)

TAYLORS CREEK METHODIST CHURCH AND CEMETERY

Taylors Creek Methodist Church was organized in 1807, by the Rev. Angus McDonald, with seven members, including James Darsey, Mrs. James Darsey and Robert Hendry.

A village soon grew up around the church, and was for many years a trading center for the surrounding area. In the cemetery adjoining the site of the church are the graves of the families of Bird, Daniels, Martin, Hendry and others who were part of the Taylors Creek community and whose names have been prominent in the history of Georgia.

The Taylors Creek Methodist Church edifice built here in 1841, was in use for 101 years, until in 1942 the site was taken over by the United States Government to become a part of the Fort Stewart area.

(Follow GA 119 north to a point 2.6 miles north of the junction with GA 144 west, turn west on unimproved road and follow for 0.2 mile to church. GHM 089-18, 1957.)

MIDWAY

BUTTON GWINNETT

In this, Saint John's Parish, (now Liberty County), lived Button Gwinnett, signer of the Declaration of Independence, member of the Continental Congress, Speaker of the Assembly, and President of the Executive Council. He also was a member of the Convention that met in Savannah in October, 1776, in which he played a prominent part in drafting the first Constitution of the State of Georgia.

COURTESY, GEORGIA HISTORICAL SOCIETY

BUTTON GWINNETT (1735-1777),
SIGNER OF THE DECLARATION OF INDEPENDENCE

Born in Gloucestershire, England, in 1735, son of a Church of England vicar, Button Gwinnett came to Georgia in 1765 and acquired a store in Savannah. He shortly purchased St. Catherines Island in this parish. He moved to the island at once and engaged in farming and cattle raising. His business was transacted in Sunbury, then a thriving port.

On May 16, 1777, Mr. Gwinnett was mortally wounded in a duel fought on the outskirts of Savannah with Gen. Lachlan McIntosh, dying on May 19. Mr. Gwinnett's grave is supposedly in Savannah, but its exact location is unknown and unmarked. One of his rare autographs sold for over $50,000.

(Located on US 17/GA 25 at Midway Church. GHM 089-2, 1954.) **Note:** Button Gwinnett's grave has been located in Savannah's Colonial Park Cemetery.

KILPATRICK AND MOWER AT MIDWAY CHURCH

On Dec. 13, 1864, Murray's brigade of Kilpatrick's cavalry division (U), scouting in the right rear of Gen. Sherman's army which was then closing in on Savannah, moved south into Liberty County. After driving back the 29th Georgia Cavalry Battalion, (C), Lt. Col. Arthur Hood, which was patrolling Liberty County, Murray advanced to Midway Church. The 5th Kentucky Cavalry was sent to Sunbury to open communications with the Union blockading squadron in St. Catherine's Sound. The 9th Pennsylvania Cavalry was sent to the Altamaha River to burn the Savannah and Gulf (ACL) Railroad bridge at Doctor Town. Both missions failed. On the 14th, Kilpatrick arrived with Atkins' brigade and the 10th Wisconsin Battery. Establishing headquarters at Midway Church, he sent foraging parties east to Colonel's Island, south below Riceboro, and west beyond the railroad to strip the country of livestock and provisions. On the 15th, with loaded wagons and herds of horses, mules and cattle, he returned to Bryan County and went into camp at "Cross Roads" (Richmond Hill).

On the 17th, Mower's division, 17th Corps (U), enroute to destroy the railroad from McIntosh to the Altamaha River, halted at Midway Church for the night. Next morning, Mower marched to McIntosh and began his destruction. Hazen's division, 15th Corps, destroyed the railroad from the Ogeechee to McIntosh.

(Located on US 17/GA 25 at Midway Church. GHM 089-25, 1959.)

SUNBURY AND FORT MORRIS

The old town of Sunbury, 11 miles East on this Road, was a leading port, said to rival Savannah in commercial importance. It was the first Seat of Justice of Liberty County. Sunbury Academy, established in 1788, was in its time the most famous School in South Georgia. The Rev. Dr. William McWhir, friend of George Washington, was Principal of the Academy for 30 years.

Fort Morris, about 350 yards south of Sunbury, was an important post during the Revolution. It was here that Col. John McIntosh sent his famous reply, "Come and take it," to the British order to surrender the fort.

(Located on US 17/GA 25 at Midway Church. GHM 089-14, 1957.)

OLD SUNBURY ROAD

The highway entering here is the Sunbury Road which once served as an arterial vehicular route from the interior of Georgia to the Town of Sunbury, a former leading port and educational center, located 11 miles to the eastward on the Midway River. The stretch from this area to Sunbury was opened about 1760.

MIDWAY CHURCH

In the early 1790's the thorough-fare was extended to Greensboro via Swainsboro and Sparta. The old way was noted for its elevated course and few stream crossings. The route declined in importance when Sunbury lost commercial significance.

(Located on US 17/GA 25 at Midway Church. GHM 089-8, 1956.)

ROAD TO SUNBURY
1734

Important Colonial Port of Entry. First Masonic Lodge meeting in Georgia believed held here February 1734, with Oglethorpe as Master.

(Located on US 17/GA 25 at Midway Church. ACH 089-99, 1930.)

ROAD TO FORT MORRIS

Constructed of heavy earthwork built by slave labor, 1776, garrisoned by Continental troops. Scene of spirited resistance to British forces.

(Located on US 17/GA 25 at Midway Church. ACH 089-91, 1930)
♦ ★ – not standing.

MIDWAY CHURCH

Built in 1792. Replaced Colonial Meeting House. Burned by British in 1778. Sherman's cavalry camped here in 1864. Midway Settlement produced many of Georgia's most Famous Men.

(Located on US 17/GA 25 at Midway Church. ACH 089-98, 1930.)

COURTESY, GEORGIA HISTORICAL SOCIETY

LYMAN HALL (1724-1790),
SIGNER OF THE DECLARATION OF INDEPENDENCE

DR. LYMAN HALL

Dr. Lyman Hall was a Georgia signer of the Declaration of Independence. He represented Saint John's Parish in the Continental Congress, and was a delegate from Georgia to the Second Continental Congress Meeting in Philadelphia.

He was a founder of Sunbury and as Governor of Georgia (1783-1784) he gave strong support to education and religion. He was instrumental in obtaining the grant of land which led to the establishment of the University of Georgia.

Born in Wallingford, Connecticut, April 12, 1724, Dr. Hall moved to Saint John's Parish where he purchased the plantation now known as Hall's Knoll. He became a leading physician, planter, patriot, and was active in Mercantile and shipping circles in Sunbury.

Dr. Hall died in 1790 and was buried on his plantation at Shell Bluff Landing in Burke County. In 1848, his remains were re-interred in Augusta, beneath the granite obelisk, "The Signers' Monument."

(Located on US 17/GA 25 at Midway Church. DAC 089-97.)

THE CEMETERY AT MIDWAY CHURCH

SAVANNAH – NEW INVERNESS ROAD
1736

This highway follows an old colonial road constructed in 1736 as a measure of defense against the Spanish and Spanish Indians by connecting rhe fighting Scotch Highlanders at New Inverness (now Darien) with Savannah. It was surveyed and cleared by soldiers and Indians furnished by Tomo-Chi-Chi under the direction of Capt. Hugh MacKay by order of Gen. James Oglethorpe. The road was travelled by such famous Georgians as Button Gwinnett, Dr. Lyman Hall, and John and Joseph LeConte.

(Located on US 17/GA 25 across from Midway Church. WPA 089-C6.)

THE REV. MR. JOHN OSGOOD

This is the grave of the Rev. Mr. John Osgood, who came to Midway with the first settlers in 1754 from Dorchester, S.C., and served them faithfully as their minister and friend until his final sermon, May 5, 1773. Born in Dorchester, one of their own people, Mr. Osgood received part of his education from their old pastor, the Rev. Mr. Fisher, and was graduated from Harvard in 1733. Ordained to the pastoral charge of the Congregational Church November 24, 1735, the Rev. Mr. Osgood ministered to these people, in Dorchester and in Midway, for 38 years. He died on August 2, 1773.

(Located on US 17/GA 25 in the cemetery across from Midway Church. GHM 089-12B, 1957.)

MIDWAY MUSEUM

MIDWAY MUSEUM

Established by South Carolina Calvinists of English and Scottish extraction in 1752, the small settlement of Midway became "the cradle of Revolutionary spirit in Georgia." Two of Georgia's three signers of the Declaration of Independence, Lyman Hall and Button Gwinnett, were sons of Midway, as were four Revolutionary Governors of the young state.

Exhibits, documents and furnishings housed in the Midway Museum commemorate and reanimate the love of liberty which distinguished the Midway Society from the Colonial period through its last meeting in December 1865.

Built in 1957, the Museum is owned and administered by the Midway Museum, Inc., organized by the Saint John's Parish Chapter, Daughters of the American Colonists and by the Liberty County Chapter, United Daughters of the Confederacy.

(Located on US 17/GA 25 in front of the Midway Museum. DAC 089-90, 1990.)

"HALL'S KNOLL" HOME OF DR. LYMAN HALL

Home-site of Dr. Lyman Hall, signer of the Declaration of Independence, member of the First Continental Congress, Governor of Georgia, member of Midway Congregational Church near here, Graduate of Yale University, (1747). Born in Wallingford, Conn., April 12, 1724, Dr. Hall moved to the Puritan Colony at Dorchester, S.C. in 1757 and after those Puritans had established themselves here in Saint John's Parish in the Province of Georgia, he moved to this place and became the leading physician of his time. He died Oct. 19, 1790, and was buried on a bluff overlooking the Savannah River. In 1848 his body was re-interred in Augusta with that of George Walton, another Georgia signer of the Declaration of Independence, beneath the Signers Monument, a granite obelisk.

Saint John's Parish was later named Liberty County in commemoration of the patriotism of the Midway Colonists here, who, from the passage of the Stamp Act, became the most uncompromising champions of liberty, and, who, in advance of the remainder of the Province, took radical action by sending Dr. Lyman Hall to the Continental Congress in Philadelphia as a delegate before the Province at large could be induced to join the federation.

(Located on US 17/GA 25, 1 mile north of Midway Church. GHM 089-1, 1954.)

LYMAN HALL PLANTATION
1778

Home of Dr. Lyman Hall (born Connecticut, 1724), Signer of Declaration of Independence, Home destroyed by British in 1778. Famous for cultivation of rice.

(Located on US 17/GA 25, 1 mile north of Midway Church. ACH 089-95, 1930.) ♦ ★ – not standing.

GENERAL JAMES SCREVEN KILLED IN BATTLE HERE

On November 24, 1778, General James Screven was mortally wounded in a battle fought near this spot.

With General Screven in the action were Major James Jackson, Colonel John White, Capt. Celerine Brusard and Capt. Edward Young, with 100 Continentals and 20 Mounted Militia, against a force of 400 British Regulars, Refugees and Indians under Col. James Mark Prevost and Col. Daniel McGirth. General Screven died from his wounds the following day.

(Located on US 17/GA 25, 1.3 miles south of Midway. GHM 089-17, 1957.)

SPENCER HILL
1778

Battleground where November 22, 1778, General James Screven was mortally wounded attempting to check British forces under General Prevost from reaching Savannah.

(Located on US 17/GA 25, 1.3 miles south of Midway. ACH 089-94, 1930.) ♦ ★ – not standing.

DORCHESTER ACADEMY

Formal education of blacks started with the Freedmen's Bureau in Liberty County. The Homestead School was continued with the aid of the American Missionary Association (AMA) and support of Reconstruction legislator William A. Golding. The AMA started with one acre of land and 77 students in 1870. In 1874, the Reverend Floyd Snelson succeeded Golding at the school. The AMA and Snelson built a new school and named it Dorchester Academy in honor of its Puritan lineage. In 1890, Dorchester Academy started a boarding school. By 1917, the school had eight frame buildings on 105 acres, 300 students, and become a fully accredited high school.

The academic program ceased in 1940, with the construction of a consolidated public school for black youth at Riceboro. All academic equipment plus $8,000 were transferred toward that consolidation. Since, the facilities have served the community under the title Dorchester Cooperative Center, Inc. AMA continues financial report.

(Located on US 84/GA 38, 1.9 miles west of junction with US 17/GA 25. GHM 089-26, 1983.)

STUDENTS OF DORCHESTER ACADEMY, 1919

DORCHESTER ACADEMY
BOY'S DORMITORY

This Georgian Revival building, built in 1934 to replace an earlier structure destroyed by fire, was once a part of an extensive school campus begun in 1871 by the American Missionary Association. The school, founded to serve the educational needs of black children of Liberty County and coastal Georgia, closed in 1940 after public education became available to black children.

In 1948 the American Missionary Association, with the assistance of the local community, expanded the

DORCHESTER ACADEMY BUILDINGS, 1927

dormitory into a community center, which by 1961 would become the focus for many activities associated with the Civil Rights Movement. The Southern Christian Leadership Conference sponsored Citizen Education Workshops here (1962-1964)., training over 1,000 teachers and leaders, who in turn educated over 10,000 in the basics of voter registration and non-violent social change. Dr. M.L. King, Jr. held a planning retreat here in 1962 to prepare for the 1963 Birmingham Campaign, one of the first major victories of the Civil Rights Movement.

(Located on US 84/GA 38, 1.9 miles west of junction with US 17/GA 25. GHM 089-27, 1990.)

DORCHESTER VILLAGE

The village of Dorchester was settled in 1843, by families from Midway and Sunbury. It was named for the Dorchesters in England, Massachusetts and South Carolina, ancestral homes of the Midway people.

Among the early settlers of the village were: Captain Abiel Winn, Capt. Cyrus Mallard, Dr. Edward J. Delegal, B.S. Busbee, W.S. Baker, Dr. Benjamin King, William Thompson, John L. Mallard, Thomas Mallard, Benjamin Allen, Dr. Troup Maxwell, William Stevens, Henry Jones and Dr. Raymond Harris.

(Located on GA 38, 5.8 miles east of Midway Church. GHM 089-19, 1957.)

DORCHESTER PRESBYTERIAN CHURCH

This church, built in 1854 on a lot of four acres donated by B.A. Busbee, was first used for summer services only. On January 6, 1871, it was admitted into the Savannah Presbytery as an organized church of 14 members. The Rev. J. W. Montgomery was the first pastor. L. J. Mallard was the first ruling elder. The bell, from old Sunbury, was once used for church, school, market and town. The font and communion service are from Midway Church. The font was a gift from Dr. William McWhir, the tankard from John Lambert, the communion service from Simon Monroe, Esq. Elders contributing most in later years – Preston Waite and Charles B. Jones.

(Follow GA 38 5.8 miles east of Midway Church until the Dorchester Village marker is located. Marker is located 0.3 miles south on unimproved road from Dorchester Village Marker. GHM 089-11, 1957.)

RICEBORO

RICEBOROUGH

Near the old North Newport Bridge, a short distance East of here, the Court House Square for Liberty County was laid out by Act of the Georgia Legislature of February 1, 1797. Riceborough was then the Seat of Justice for Liberty County, and a Court House and Public Buildings were erected here on land given by Matthew McAllister, Esq. Thomas Stevens, Daniel Stewart, Joel Walker and Henry Wood were named Commissioners.

Riceborough was for many years an important port for the shipping of rice and other agricultural products from this area.

(Located on US 17/GA 25 near the junction with GA 119. GHM 089-13, 1957.)

LeCONTE BOTANICAL GARDENS

Five miles west of here on the old Post Road, the southernmost postal route in America, is the site of the home and botanical gardens of Louis LeConte, naturalist, mathematician and scholar, for whom the famous LeConte Pear was named. A native of New Jersey, Dr. LeConte was married to Ann Quarterman, a member of Midway Church in 1812. He established his famed botanical gardens on his extensive plantation. In his attic he fitted a chemical laboratory which included novelties of a botanical garden in which he cultivated rare plants, which came from all parts of the world. Although the modest Dr. LeConte did not exploit his achievements, it was nothing unusual for visitors from foreign lands to view his gardens.

Dr. LeConte's internationally known sons, Dr. John LeConte, born in 1818 and Dr. Joseph LeConte, born in 1823, at the family plantation, were two of the most distinguished scientific scholars of the nineteenth century. They made the University of California famous.

(Located on US 17/GA 25, 2.3 miles north. GHM 089-3, 1954.)

WILLIAM BARTRAM TRAIL
Traced 1773-1777

In 1773 William Bartram, here Viewed Woodmanston Plantation, Later the home of his friend, Naturalist John E. LeConte.

(From US 17/GA 25, 2.3 miles north of Riceboro at the LeConte Botanical Gardens Marker follow the intersecting road for 4 miles, then continue straight on dirt road for 0.9 mile to Marker. The LeConte Garden site is 0.9 mile down the intersecting road from the Marker. GCG 089-92, 1983.)

SKIRMISH IN
BULLTOWN SWAMP

In November of 1778, Lieut. Col. James Mark Prevost, with 100 British Regulars, and 300 Refugees and Indians under McGirth, crossed the Altamaha River and moved into Georgia, killing or taking prisoner all men they found, and ravaging the plantations. Continental troops and Militia marched against them. Near this spot, where the old Savannah to Darien road crossed Bulltown Swamp, a small detachment of Mounted Militia, Col. John Baker commanding, met and fought a delaying action with the invaders. Colonel Baker, Captain Cooper and William Goulding were wounded.

(Located on US 17/GA 25, 6 miles south of Riceboro. GHM 089-16, 1957.)

SIMON MUNRO

In the family cemetery on this plantation, Westfield, Simon Munro, donor of the silver communion service used for many years in old Midway Congregational Church, is buried. Early in the Revolutionary War, Simon Munro, a resident of St. John's Parish, was banished from the State of Georgia, and forbidden to set foot within its borders, because of his Tory activities. After repeated petitions from his friends and neighbors, the banishment was lifted and he was allowed to return to his home and family.

(Follow US 17/GA 25, 2.9 miles south, take paved road west, at 4.3 miles continue through junction for an additional 1.3 miles to marker. GHM 089-23, 1958.)

CEDAR HILL

Colonial plantation home of General Daniel Stewart, Revolutionary patriot and maternal great-grandfather of President Theodore Roosevelt.

(Located on US 17/GA 25 in Riceboro. ACH 089-93, 1930.) ♦ ★ – not standing.

SUNBURY

SUNBURY

Now numbered among the Dead Towns of Georgia, old Sunbury was once a great seaport, said to rival Savannah in commercial importance. Laid out in 1758, on a tract of 350 acres conveyed by Mark Carr for the purpose to James Maxwell, Kenneth Baillie, John Elliott, Grey Elliott and John Stevens, as Trustees, the town contained 496 lots and embraced three squares – King's, Church and Meeting. The first session of Superior Court in Liberty County was held in Sunbury, Nov. 18, 1783, and it remained the County Seat until 1797.

Sunbury Academy, established by the Legislature in 1788, with Abiel Holmes, James Dunwody, John Elliott, Gideon Dowse and Peter Winn as Commissioners, was for many years the most famous school in South Georgia. For nearly 30 years its Principal was the Rev. Dr. William McWhir, friend of George Washington and a former principal of the Academy of Alexandria, Va. Among other teachers of Sunbury Academy were: the Rev. Thomas Goulding, Uriah Wilcox, the Rev. A. T. Holmes, the Rev. S. G. Hilyer, Major John Winn, W. T. Feay and Oliver W. Stevens.

(Located off GA 38, 0.5 mile past the entrance to the Sunbury Historic Site. GHM 089-15, 1957.)

SUNBURY
HOME OF MANY FAMOUS PERSONS

Many famous persons lived in the town of Sunbury. Among them was Dr. Lyman Hall, signer of the Declaration of Independence. It was also the home of Richard Howley and Nathan Brownson, later governors of Georgia; of John Elliott and Alfred Cuthbert, United States Senators; of Major John Jones and Major Lachlan McIntosh. Button Gwinnett, another signer of the Declaration of Independence, spent much time here as a Justice of St. John's Parish, and Georgia's third signer, George Walton, was among those held in Sunbury as a prisoner of the British during the Revolution.

Maria J. McIntosh, noted authoress, and her brother, Commodore James McKay McIntosh, hero of the Mexican War, were born in Sunbury. The Hon. John E. Ward, first United States Minister to China, and the Hon. William Law, noted Jurist, were also natives of Sunbury.

(Located off GA 38, 0.5 mile past the entrance to the Sunbury Historic Site. GHM 089-4B, 1957.)

SAINT JOHN'S LODGE NUMBER SIX

Saint John's Lodge Number Six , of Sunbury, Free and accepted Masons, was chartered by the Grand Lodge of Georgia, April 21, 1777, in Masonry 5777. Under an act of the Legislature of Georgia, February 6, 1796, The Grand Lodge was incorporated and given power to corporate bodies under their jurisdiction. Under this new authority, the Grand Lodge, on June 5, 1802 "On motion ordered that Saint John's Lodge Number Six, Sunbury hold their charter on paying arrearage due.

Annual returns were made to the Grand Lodge back to 1787 and the Lodge was admitted to full participation with the following officers recognized: Adam Alexander, Worshipful Master; William Peacock, Senior Warden; Andrew Maybank, Junior Warden; Thomas Lancaster, Treasurer; Daniel Stewart, Secretary; Nathan Dryer, Senior Deacon; John Bihlheimer, Junior Deacon; James Robarts, Steward; Samuel Law, Steward; and George C. Somerall, Tyler.

On November 4, 1805, John and Rebecca Couper gave to the lodge, lot No. 77 of the Town of Sunbury, situate a few hundred feet north of the marker, upon which to erect a Lodge building.

(Located off GA 38, 0.5 mile past the entrance to the Sunbury Historic Site. GLG 089-96, 1957.)

SUNBURY CEMETERY

In this Cemetery are buried men and women whose lives contributed much to the early history of Georgia.

Among these were the Rev. Wm. McWhir, D.D., and his wife. The Rev. Mr. McWhir was for 30 years Principal of the famous Sunbury Academy. Born in Ireland, September 9, 1759, he was graduated from

COURTESY, GEORGIA HISTORICAL SOCIETY

WILLIAM McWHIR
(1759-1851)

Belfast College and was licensed to preach by the presbytery of that City. He died in Georgia, January 30, 1851.

Some burials were made in this plot in Colonial and Revolutionary Days, but most of the markers had been destroyed before the 1870's.

(Located in the cemetery. Drive 0.5 mile past the entrance to the Sunbury Historic Site, at fork, bear left on dirt road for 0.2 mile, turn left 0.1 mile, turn right 0.1 mile to cemetery. GHM 089-20, 1957.)

FORT MORRIS

Erected at the beginning of the Revolutionary War, to guard the Port of Sunbury and St. John's Parish, Fort Morris was an enclosed earthwork in the shape of an irregular quadrangle. Surrounded by a parapet and moat, it contained a parade of about an acre.

SUNBURY CEMETERY

The fort was defended by more than 25 pieces of ordnance of various size. It was named in honor of Captain Morris, who commanded the company of artillery by which it was first garrisoned early in 1776.

Colonel John McIntosh commanded the garrison on November 25, 1778, when Col. L. V. Fuser, with 500 British ground troops, supported by armed ships in the Medway river, landed at Sunbury and demanded the immediate surrender of Fort Morris. Colonel McIntosh, with 127 Continental troops, some militia and citizens of Sunbury, less than 200 men in all, replied, "Come and Take it!"

The enemy retreated to the South, and Continental troops held Fort Morris until January 9, 1779, when it was captured by British forces.

(Located at Sunbury Historic Site, in front of the visitor's center. GHM 089-12A, 1957.)

McINTOSH COUNTY

Named in honor of the distinguished McIntosh family. Captain John McIntosh Mohr was the leader of the Scots who in 1736, settled in Darien. County Seat: Darien.

CRESCENT

BAISDEN'S BLUFF ACADEMY

Located a short distance East of here, near the River, Baisden's Bluff Academy was the main educational institution in McIntosh County in the early years of the 19th century. A Boarding School, operating the year round, its roll held the names of prominent families of this county and from adjoining areas. "Mr. Linder" was Principal. General Francis Hopkins, Wm. A. Dunham, James Dunwoody, James Smith and Jacob Wood were Commissioners.

In 1823 torrential rains washed the dormitory into the river, leaving a ravine which can still be seen. The school never recovered.

(Located on GA 99, 12.2 miles east of US 17/GA 25. GHM 095-12, 1957.)

GOVERNOR GEORGE M. TROUP
(1780-1856)

OLD BELLEVILLE OR TROUP CEMETERY

Within these walls are buried Captain Troup, British Naval officer, and his wife, Catherine McIntosh Troup. They were the parents of George M. Troup, Governor of Georgia 1823-1827; U.S. Senator 1829-1833. It was on this plantation that George M. Troup spent his early boyhood.

Ten other graves lie within this enclosure; the inscriptions on the marble slabs which marked them were effaced by time before 1850.

(From GA 99 in Crescent, take the road to Pelican Point 2 miles to dead end, turn left on dirt road for 0.5 mile. GHM 095-34, 1957. **Note:** Worth a special trip – this cemetery has almost been lost in time.)

DARIEN

McINTOSH COUNTY

This county, created Dec. 19, 1793 from Liberty County, was named for the McIntosh family, early settlers, whose name was associated with most events in Georgia history for many years. John McIntosh, with 170 Highlanders, came to Georgia in January 1735 and founded Darien. George N. Ragan was made Tax Collector of McIntosh County Dec. 23, 1793. County officers, commissioned March 25, 1794, were: William Middleton, Sheriff; John Baillie, Clerk of Superior and Inferior Courts; John Richey, Coroner; George N. Ragan, Surveyor. Joseph Clark was commissioned Tax Receiver, Dec. 21, 1794.

(Located on US 17/GA 25 on the court house lawn. GHM 095-5, 1956.)

OGLETHORPE OAK 1736

Traditional site of Oglethorpe's shelter in 1736 upon occasion of his visit to Darien, a town founded that year by Scotchmen under his direction.

(Located on US 17/GA 25 on the court house lawn. ACH 095-99, 1930.) **Note:** The tree is not standing but was measured in 1895 as follows: Height – 75 feet, Circumference – 360 feet, Trunk – 15 feet, 6 inches.

DARIEN

This is Darien, in the heart of the historic Altamaha delta region. Settled in 1736, by Scottish Highlanders under John McIntosh Mohr, it was named for the ill-fated settlement on the Isthmus of Panama. The first military parade in Georgia was held in Darien, February 22, 1736, when Gen. James Edward Oglethorpe reviewed the Highland Company in full regalia, with claymores, side arms and targes. The Highland Company supported Oglethorpe in all his campaigns, and won everlasting fame on the field of Bloody Marsh. During the Revolution, Darien men again came to the front – Gen. Lachlan McIntosh, Col. Wm. McIntosh and Col. John McIntosh were among the heroes of that War. In 1818 the City of Darien was chartered, and became the County Seat. The Bank of Darien, chartered in 1818, was the strongest Bank south of Philadelphia, with branches in 7 Georgia cities. Huge mills sawed into lumber millions of feet of timber rafted down the river. Darien was one of the great ports of the Eastern Seaboard. It was burned in 1863 by Northern troops stationed on St. Simon's Island. Rebuilt in the 1870's, Darien again became a great port, and the mills sawed lumber to be shipped all over the world. Depletion of the forests brought this era to an end in the early 1900's.

(Located on US 17/GA 25 at the Altamaha River bridge. GHM 095-30, 1957.)

FORT KING GEORGE

The site of Fort King George, first fort on Georgia soil, built by the English. Erected by the Colony of South Carolina in 1721, 12 years before the Georgia Colony was founded.

This fort served as a barrier against the Spanish in Florida, French in the interior, and their Indian allies, for about a decade.

Soldiers, who died in service, are buried nearby in a graveyard, lost for 200 years. Some of the graves are marked now. Others are on the site of a 16th century Spanish Mission.

(Located on US 17/GA 25 at the Altamaha River bridge. GHM 095-6A, 1952.)

FORT DARIEN

Fort Darien, laid out by General James Edward Oglethorpe in 1736, was built on this first high bluff of the Altamaha river to protect the new town of Darien. It was a large fortification, with two bastions and 2 half bastions, and was defended by several cannon.

From the time of its settlement by Scottish Highlanders in 1736, until after the Battle of Bloody Marsh in 1742, the town of Darien was in constant danger from the Spaniards of Florida. Often for weeks at a time the Highland soldiers were absent from home on military campaigns, with only a few men left to guard the women and children who, for safety, lived within the walls of the fort. On several occasions the post was fired upon by Spaniards or their Indian allies.

After the War with Spain was ended, the fort, no longer needed, fell into ruins, but was rebuilt and armed during the Revolution, when it again saw action, this time against British forces.

(Located on US 17/GA 25 at the Altamaha River bridge. GHM 095-18, 1957.)

GENERAL'S ISLAND

This island was the property of General Lachlan McIntosh by a grant of 1758, and was the principal home of his family up to and during the early years of the Revolution. The island was in rice cultivation for many years.

In 1808, a Canal, called General's Cut, was dug through the Island to connect the Darien River with the middle branch of the Altamaha, "for the convenience of the adjoining planters."

This Cut, located a short distance east of here, was later used to ferry between Darien and the southern plantations of the Delta.

Located on US 17/GA 25, 0.8 mile south of Darien. GHM 095-23, 1957.)

FRANCES ANNE (FANNY) KEMBLE, (MRS. PIERCE BUTLER)
(1809-1893)

FAMOUS BUTLER AUTHORS

Pierce Butler and his daughter, Frances, who shared his interest in the South, returned to Butler Island in 1866, and worked to rehabilitate the plantations. Pierce Butler died in 1867, but Frances continued for several years to manage the Island acreage. She wrote a book, "Ten Years On a Georgia Plantation," an interesting and valuable account of life in this section during the Reconstruction. Owen Wister, famous author of "The Virginian," and other novels, was the son of Sarah Butler, sister of Frances. He often visited Butler Island plantation.

(Located on US 17/GA 25, 1.3 miles south of Darien. GHM 095-9, 1957.)

MILL CHIMNEY AT BUTLER ISLAND PLANTATION

BUTLER ISLAND PLANTATION

Famous Rice Plantation of the 19th century, owned by Pierce Butler of Philadelphia. A system of dikes and canals for the cultivation of rice, installed by engineers from Holland, is still in evidence in the old fields, and has been used as a pattern for similar operations in recent years.

During a visit here with her husband in 1839-40, Pierce Butler's wife, the brilliant English actress, Fannie Kemble, wrote her "Journal of a Residence On A Georgia Plantation," which is said to have influenced England against the Confederacy.

(Located on US 17/GA 25, 1.3 miles south of Darien. GHM 095-25, 1957.)

BUTLER'S ISLAND

Ante-bellum rice plantation where Frances H. (Fanny) Kemble (Mrs. Pierce Butler), celebrated English actress, in 1838-39 wrote Diary, published in 1863, which helped turn English sentiment against Confederacy.

(Located on US 17/GA 25, 1.3 miles south of Darien. ACH 095-98, 1930.) ♦ ★ – not standing.

OLD SPANISH MISSION

This road leads to a Franciscan Mission established before English founded Jamestown. Flourished for a century. Indians murdered its missionary in Yemassee revolt of 1596. Bishop of Cuba preached here in 1606.

(Located on US 17/GA 25 in Darien. ACH 095-96, 1930.) ♦ ★ – not standing.

ROAD TO ST. SIMON'S ISLAND
BATTLEFIELD OF BLOODY MARSH
OLD FORT FREDERICA
JOHN WESLEY OAK

(Located on US 17/GA 25 south of Darien. ACH 095-97, 1930.) ♦ ★ – not standing.

SAINT ANDREW'S EPISCOPAL CHURCH

Saint Andrew's Episcopal Church in Darien received its charter in 1843, under the Rt. Rev. Stephen Elliott, first Bishop of the Diocese of Georgia. The church edifice, a large wooden building with a belfry, erected on a lot a short distance North of this site, was completed in 1844. The Rev. Richard Brown was the first Rector.

This building was burned in 1863, when Darien was put to the torch by Federal troops stationed on St. Simon's Island, and for several years after services were held in a little church on The Ridge.

In 1872, James K. Clarke, Mr. Langdon and Donald Munroe headed a movement to rebuild Saint Andrew's in Darien. Other members of the church assisted with money and with work. Plans were secured from England, and the edifice as it now stands, a copy of a little church in Britain, was built.

The church was opened in January of 1879, with the Rev. Samuel Pinkerton as Rector.

(Located east of US 17/GA 25 on Washington Street at Vernon Square. GHM 095-7, 1957. **Note:** The church building had been in use for seven years prior to 1879.)

SITE OF BANK OF DARIEN

The old Bank of Darien, in its day the strongest Bank South of Philadelphia, was organized in 1818 with a Capital Stock of $1,000,000. The first Directors on the part of the State were: Thomas Spalding, Scott Cray, John McIntosh, James Troup, James Dunwoody; for the Stock-

holders: Calvin Baker, Barrington King, John Kell, Henry Harford, Jonathan Sawyer.

With Branches in Savannah, Macon, Milledgeville, Marion, Dahlonega, Auraria and Augusta, the Bank of Darien was a powerful force in Agricultural and Commercial activities in Georgia. It also financed the gold fields of North Georgia and North Carolina.

An important factor in the economy of the South, the Bank was at one time the depository for $1,400,000 in Federal Revenues.

The Bank of Darien became deeply involved in politics, and during the latter years of its operation was the center of bitter controversy. Its charter was terminated by the State Legislature in 1841.

(Located east of US 17/GA 25 on Washington Street at Vernon Square. GHM 095-8, 1957.)

SAINT CYPRIAN'S EPISCOPAL CHURCH

Saint Cyprian's Episcopal Church in Darien was built "for the Colored People of McIntosh County," through the efforts of the Rev. James Wentworth Leigh, D.D., F.S.A., Dean of Hereford, England. It was named for the martyred African Bishop.

Contributions toward the building of the church edifice were received from England, Philadelphia and from local citizens. Members of the congregation, led by the Senior Warden, Lewis Jackson, gave devotedly of their time and labor.

Saint Cyprian's church edifice was consecrated Sunday April 30, 1876, by the Rt. Rev. John W. Beckwith, Bishop of Georgia, and placed under the guardianship of Saint Andrew's Episcopal Church in Darien, of which the Rev. Robert Clute was then Rector.

(Located at Fort King George Drive and Rittenhouse Street. GHM 095-26, 1957.)

200 YEARS OF SAWMILLING

For nearly two centuries the story of sawmilling in the Southeast was enacted on this point on the Altamaha River. In the summer of 1721, men from South Carolina sawed the 3-inch planks to build Fort King George. In 1736, indentured servants of the Scottish Highlanders set up pit saws here and sawed lumber for the permanent houses of Darien and for public buildings in Savannah and Frederica. This was the first commercial manufacture of lumber in Coastal Georgia. Through the years, sawmilling continued on this site. In the latter part of the 18th century, a large water mill was constructed and used here, operated by impounding tidal water in a basin on flood tide and sawing with the ebb.

In 1818, the Darien Eastern Steam Sawmill was built here. Designed by an engineer from London, the mill had five gang saws. In use, with brief

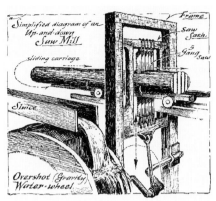

FROM A REVERENCE FOR WOOD. "UP AND DOWN SAW MILL" BY ERIC SLOANE

interruptions, until about 1905, it was then dismantled because of lack of large timber. A circular sawmill, built alongside the same basin, took its place, to be used until the end of the sawmill era in Darien.

(Located on the grounds of Fort King George, at the end of Fort King George Drive. GHM 095-6B, 1957.)

SITE OF EARLY SPANISH MISSION

This high bluff was the site of one of the early Spanish Missions of the old District of Guale. Here, in the late 16th and the 17th centuries, Franciscan friars labored with the Indians, converting them to Christianity and instructing them in agriculture and other crafts of civilization.

Occupied by a large Indian village before the coming of the Spaniards, this tract was an ideal site for the mission and school activities of the Spanish priests. Archaeological excavations in the area in 1941 and 1953 disclosed evidence of both Indian and Spanish occupation –

Indian pottery and bone tools with Spanish olive jars, majolica and iron work, outlines of buildings constructed before and after the coming of white men.

Built in the area called by the Spaniards, "Talaje," the mission on this site was part of a chain of missions and visitas by which Spain held title for nearly two centuries to what is now the Coast of Georgia.

(Located on the grounds of Fort King George, at the end of Fort King George Drive. GHM 095-10, 1957.)

OLD FORT KING GEORGE

Site of old Fort King George, built in 1721 by Col. John Barnwell, of South Carolina, under British Royal orders. This tiny cypress blockhouse, 26 feet square, with 3 floors, and a lookout in the gable from which the guard could watch over the Inland Waterway and St. Simons Island, was flanked by officers quarters and barracks, and the entire area was surrounded on all but the river side by a moat and palisades. Garrisoned by his Majesty's Independent Company, with replacements of Colony scouts, the fort was occupied for six years. During that time more than 140 officers and soldiers lost their lives here and were buried on the adjacent bluff. The first of the British 18th century scheme of posts built to counteract French expansion in America, Fort King George was also a flagrant trespass upon Spanish territory, and during its occupation Spain continually demanded that it be destroyed.

A RECONSTRUCTION OF THE OLD FORT KING GEORGE BLOCKHOUSE

The troops were withdrawn to Port Royal in 1727, but until Oglethorpe arrived in Savannah in 1733 South Carolina kept two lookouts at old Fort King George.

(Located on the grounds of Fort King George, at the end of Fort King George Drive. GHM 095-19, 1957.)

BIRTHPLACE OF JOHN McINTOSH KELL

Laurel Grove, at the end of this avenue, was the birthplace of John McIntosh Kell, 1823-1900, distinguished Naval officer. He was a member of the expedition of Commodore Matthew C. Perry to Japan in 1853, and was Master of the flagship *Mississippi* on the homeward cruise. When Georgia seceded from the Union, John McIntosh Kell resigned his commission to join the Confederacy. He was Executive Officer of the *Sumter*; then of the *Alabama* throughout her brilliant career on the seas, and in her final battle with the *Kearsarge* off Cherbourg. Later in life, John McIntosh Kell served for several

COURTESY, GEORGIA DEPARTMENT OF INDUSTRY AND TRADE

JOHN McINTOSH KELL
(1823-1900)

COURTESY, GEORGIA HISTORICAL SOCIETY

THOMAS SPALDING
(1774-1851)

years as Adjutant General of the State of Georgia.

(Located on GA 99, 0.8 mile east of US 17/GA 25 and near Old Fort King George. GHM 095-36, 1958.)

ST. ANDREW'S CEMETERY

At the end of this avenue, on high land overlooking the creeks and marshes, Thomas Spalding of Sapelo established his family burial ground. For many years the Spaldings and their kinsmen were buried there.

In 1867, Charles Spalding, son of Thomas Spalding, gave to Saint

Andrew's Episcopal Church in Darien the land surrounding the family plot, to be used perpetually as a cemetery. On February 20, 1876, the Right Reverend Dr. Beckwith, Bishop of Georgia, consecrated the ground now known as St. Andrew's Cemetery.

(Located on GA 99, 1.4 miles east of US 17/GA 25. GHM 095-15, 1957.)

"THE THICKET"
SUGAR MILL – RUM DISTILLERY RUINS

On the banks of Carnochan Creek, a short distance east of here, are the ruins of a famous Sugar Mill and Rum Distillery operated early in the 19th century.

"THE THICKET" SLAVE QUARTER RUINS

These buildings, constructed of tabby by William Carnochan on his huge sugar plantation at "The Thicket," followed closely plans laid out by Thomas Spalding of Sapelo. The sugar works and rum distillery were operated successfully on a commercial scale until 1824, when a hurricane tore off the roof and upper story of the mill and cane barn, and destroyed other buildings.

(Located on GA 99, 5.4 miles east of US 17/GA 25 near Ridgeville. GHM 095-27, 1957.)

DARIEN PRESBYTERIAN CHURCH

Darien was the Cradle of Presbyterianism in Georgia, as the first Presbyterian church in the Colony was established by Scottish Highlanders who settled this town in January, 1736. The Scots brought with them their minister, the Rev. John McLeod, of the Isle of Skye. Immediately upon their arrival at what is now Lower Bluff, one mile East of this site, they built a Chapel for Divine Worship, and there the Rev. John McLeod preached during his ministry in Darien.

Later, the Meeting House was built about eight miles North of Darien on the Savannah road, to serve the people of St. Andrew's Parish, at that time almost entirely Presbyterian.

In 1808 the First Presbyterian Church of Darien received its charter, and a building was erected near the center of the town. This was later burned, and for a time services were held in another building in the vicinity.

A place of worship, built on this site and dedicated in January of 1876, was later destroyed by fire. The present edifice was constructed in 1900.

(Located west of US 17/GA 25 at Jackson and West Third Streets. GHM 095-28, 1957.)

OLD RIVER ROAD

The River Road has changed but little in location since its beginning as a Military Route in 1739. Scottish Highlanders first marched over it on their way to invade Spanish Florida, and troops have used it in three wars – the War with Spain, the Revolution, and the War Between the States. As a civilian highway, this served first as the road to Fort Barrington and the Ferry, later as an important link in the old Macon to Darien highway, over which planters in their carriages, stage coaches, and riders carrying the U.S. Mail, travelled during the early 19th century.

(Located on US 17/GA 25 at the junction with GA 251, 1 mile north of Darien. GHM 095-17, 1957.)

FORT BARRINGTON

Fort Barrington, about twelve miles West of here on the Altamaha River, was built in 1751. Lieut. Robert Baillie, in charge of construction, commanded the post for several years.

Named Fort Howe during the Revolution, the fort played a vital part in that War, guarding the most dangerous land pass on the Southern Frontier of Georgia. In constant peril from British forces and their Indian allies, the fort was the scene of several battles and skirmishes.

Confederate troops were stationed on the site during the War Between the States.

(Located on US 17/GA 25 at the junction with GA 251, 1 mile north of Darien. GHM 095-14, 1957.)

ARDOCH

Ardoch, fronting on the old Stage Road from Savannah to Darien where it traversed this Swamp, was the plantation home of the McDonalds from Colonial Days through the early 19th century.

During the Revolutionary War, members of this branch of the McDonald clan were Loyalists, as were many families of Coastal Georgia. In a skirmish fought in his home in Ardoch, only a short distance from this spot, Robert McDonald was killed in the presence of his wife and children, and the Ardoch house burned.

(Located on US 17/GA 25, 6.9 miles north of Darien. GHM 095-16, 1957.)

OLD MEETING HOUSE

Two hundreds yards west of this spot stood the "Old Meeting House," built before 1750 to serve the Scottish Presbyterians of the District of Darien. A landmark in Colonial days, it was in use until after the Revolutionary War, both as a church and as a meeting place for the citizens of St. Andrew's Parish on important occasions. It was here that the "Darien Committee" met on January 12, 1775, to choose their delegates to the Provincial Congress at Savannah, and to adopt the six Resolutions which are today among our treasured Revolutionary documents.

(Located on US 17/GA 25, 8.1 miles north of Darien. GHM 095-22, 1957.)

CAPTURE OF 23 OLD MEN IN 1864

Near here, in Ebenezer Church, 23 old men were captured by Federal troops on the night of August 3rd, 1864. These civilians, too old for military service, were the sole protection of McIntosh County, which was constantly being plundered by forces from blockade gunboats.

Advised of the meeting by spies, Federal troops surrounded the church in the darkness and opened fire. The old men were captured and marched overland to Blue and Hall Landing near Darien, where they were put on board ship and taken to Northern prisons.

(Located on US 17/GA 25, 8.8 miles north of Darien. GHM 095-33, 1957.)

EULONIA

OLD COURT HOUSE AT SAPELO BRIDGE

Sapelo Bridge, on the old Savannah to Darien Road 200 yards east of this spot, was the seat of McIntosh County from 1793 to 1818. Here the Court House and other public buildings stood; here, too, were the Armory and Muster Ground for the McIntosh County Cavalry Troop, and here the Stage Coaches stopped to refresh the passengers and change horses.

(Located on US 17/GA 25, 0.8 mile north. GHM 095-24, 1957.)

RICE HOPE

Famous Rice and Indigo Plantation of Colonial and Revolutionary times. Rice Hope was the home of George McIntosh, son of John McIntosh Mor of Darien, and brother of General Lachlan McIntosh. George McIntosh was Official Surveyor for St. Andrew's Parish, Member of the Commons House of Assembly, Member of the First Provincial Congress of Georgia, Member of the Council of Safety During the Revolution, the home of George McIntosh at Rice Hope was burned and his slaves and stock run off by the British.

(Located on US 17/GA 25, 2 miles north. GHM 095-21, 1957.)

JOHN HOUSTOUN McINTOSH

John Houstoun McIntosh, son of George McIntosh, was born at Rice Hope, May 1, 1773.

When a young man, he settled in East Florida and became a leader of the U.S. citizens living there. He was appointed "Governor or Director of the Republic of Florida" in 1812. After a stormy career in Florida, he returned to Georgia, and in 1818 served in the Seminole War as General in the Militia.

In 1825, he began intensive cultivation of sugar cane on his plantation in Camden County, and there installed the first horizontal sugar mill ever worked by cattle power.

(Located on US 17/GA 25, 2 miles north. GHM 095-13, 1957.)

MALLOW PLANTATION

This plantation was a Crown grant to Captain John McIntosh, a British Army officer who served in Florida during the War with Spain. Later, when this officer went into the Indian country, his brother, the eccentric Captain Roderick (Rory) McIntosh, with their sister, Miss Winnewood McIntosh, occupied the home which was built upon this bluff in the 1760's. The exploits of the redoubtable Rory have filled pages of pre-Revolutionary Georgia history.

After the Revolution, Mallow became the property of Captain William McIntosh, a son of Captain John. He, too, was a British Army officer, and was the father of the Indian Chief, General William McIntosh.

Early in the 19th century, Mallow was purchased by Mr. and Mrs. Reuben King, and they were living here when the plantation was raided by forces from a Federal gunboat anchored in nearby Sapelo River, in November, 1862.

(From Eulonia follow US 17/GA 25 north 2.2 miles, follow paved road east for 2.8 miles to Pine Harbor. GHM 095-20, 1957.)

CAPTAIN WILLIAM McINTOSH

In this plot under the "Great Oak at Mallow Plantation," Captain William McIntosh, father of the Indian chief, General William McIntosh, was buried in 1794. Captain McIntosh, an officer in the British army, when stationed in the Creek country, married two Indian women and their sons, William and Roderick, became chiefs among the Creeks.

Gen. William McIntosh was killed by his own people on May 1, 1825, for signing the Treaty of Indian Springs. Later his sons and his half-brother, Roderick (Roley) led the great Creek trek to Old Indian Territory. They and their descendants have been distinguished lawyers, ministers, statesmen, artists, soldiers – noted leaders in the building of the West.

(From Eulonia follow US 17/GA 25 north 2.2 miles, follow paved road east for 2.8 miles to Pine Harbor. Marker is south on unpaved road 0.1 mile. GHM 095-3, 1955.)

THE GREAT OAK AT MALLOW PLANTATION

COLONEL JOHN McINTOSH

About one mile from this spot, at Fairhope, the adjoining plantation, Colonel John McIntosh, a hero of the American Revolution, was buried in 1826.

It was Colonel McIntosh, in command of Fort Morris at Sunbury, who, when the British Lieut. Col. L.V. Fuser demanded the surrender of the fort on Nov. 20, 1778, replied: "Come and Take It."

A member of the family of Scottish Highlanders who led in the settlement of Darien and for whom the county of McIntosh was named, Col. McIntosh had a long and distinguished military career, serving throughout the Revolution and the War of 1812.

(From Eulonia follow US 17/GA 25 2.2 miles, follow paved road east for 2.8 miles to Pine Harbor. Marker is south on unpaved road 0.1 mile. GHM 095-4, 1955.)

SUTHERLAND'S BLUFF

Sutherland's Bluff, about 1.5 miles South on this road, overlooks the Sapelo River and the Inland Waterway. The site was named for Lieut. Patrick Sutherland, to whom it was granted, upon recommendation of General James Edward Oglethorpe, in recognition of the Lieutenant's service at the Battle of Bloody Marsh.

At the beginning of the Revolutionary War, a shipyard was laid out at Sutherland's Bluff, moulds were made at Philadelphia, and liveoak timbers were cut at the Bluff for the building of gunboats and four frigates for the Continental Navy. The British blockade of 1778 prevented the completion of the work. In the late 18th and early 19th centuries, Sutherland's Bluff was a regular stop for ships sailing the Inland Waterway, and a store and livery stable kept there for the convenience of outfitting passengers disembarking for overland travel. In 1954, archaeological investigations disclosed evidence of ancient Indian and Spanish occupation of the bluff.

(From Eulonia follow US 17/GA 25 north 2.2 miles, follow road east for 0.1 mile, turn left on Shellman Bluff Road for 6.9 miles, bear right at fork for 0.7 mile. GHM 095-35, 1958.)

SOUTH NEWPORT

CONFEDERATE POST IN 1864

Near this spot, Company F of the Third South Carolina Cavalry, Lieut. W. L. Mole commanding, was stationed during the summer of 1864. The Company was on Patrol duty, guarding the Coast of McIntosh County.

On the night of August 18th, the post was attacked by Federal Troops coming up the South Newport River. Of Company F, less than 20 men escaped death or capture. Five civilian prisoners were taken also, and the Bridge over the South Newport River was burned.

(Located on US 17/GA 25, 0.2 mile south of the South Newport River Bridge. GHM 095-32, 1957.)

SOUTH NEWPORT BAPTIST CHURCH

This Church was organized by the Rev. Charles O. Screven at Harris Neck, 7 miles West of here, during the early 1800's. As the Harris Neck Baptist Church, it was admitted to the Sunbury Baptist Association November 12, 1824.

In the early 1830's, the Church was moved to this site and became the South Newport Baptist Church. On December 9, 1841, the South Newport Baptist Church was chartered, the Trustees named: Charles W. Thorpe, Gideon B. Dean, Thomas K. Gould, William J. Cannon, Henry J. White. The present edifice is the second erected on this site.

(Located on US 17/GA 25 at the junction with GA 131, 0.4 mile south of the South Newport River Bridge. GHM 095-31, 1957.)

JONESVILLE

The site of the village of Jonesville, so named for its first settler, Samuel Jones, is about 6 miles West on this road. There, early in the Revolution, McGirth with British forces attacked a small garrison at Moses Way's stockade and a fierce battle took place, ending in the defeat of McGirth. In 1843, a Congregational Church was chartered at Jonesville, with Nathaniel Varnedoe, Wm.

MARIA J. McINTOSH
(1803-1878)

Jones and Moses L. Jones, Trustees. The village became a refuge for women, children and invalids from the Coast when that area was blockaded by Federal gunboats during the War Between the States.

(Located on US 17/GA 25, 0.6 mile south of the South Newport River Bridge. GHM 095-29, 1957.)

THE McINTOSH FAMILY OF McINTOSH COUNTY

The service of this family to America, since the first of the Clan, with their leader, Captain John McIntosh Mohr, came from the Highlands of Scotland to Georgia, in 1736, forms a brilliant record.

The roll of distinguished members of this family includes: Gen. Lachlan McIntosh, Col. William McIntosh, Col. John McIntosh, Maj. Lachlan McIntosh – officers in the Revolution; Col. James L. McIntosh, killed in the Mexican War; Maria J. McIntosh, authoress; Capt. John McIntosh, Capt. Wm. McIntosh of Mallow, Capt. Roderick (Rory) McIntosh – British Army officers serving in the War with Spain and in the Indian country; George M. Troup, Governor of Georgia; John McIntosh Kell, Second Officer of the *Alabama*; Thomas Spalding of Sapelo; Creek Indian Chiefs – Gen. Wm. McIntosh, Roley McIntosh, Judge Alexander McIntosh, Acee Blue Eagle... and many others.

(Located on US 17/GA 25, 1.7 miles south of the South Newport River Bridge. GHM 095-11, 1957.)

TOWNSEND

FORT BARRINGTON

Approximately ten miles west of here on the banks of the Altamaha River stood Fort Barrington, a stronghold whose origin dates back to earliest Colonial times. It was built as a defense against the Spaniards and Indians and was called Fort Barrington in honor of a friend and kinsman of General James Edward Oglethorpe, Lieutenant Colonel Josiah Barrington. This gentleman, a scion of the English nobility, was a large landowner in Georgia, whose home was just east of Barrington Ferry on San Savilla Bluff. Fort Barrington, which was twelve miles northwest of the town of Darien, was renamed Fort Howe during the Revolution as it fell into the hands of the British.

The fort long ago ceased to exist, but the old military road which formerly ran between Savannah and Fort Barrington is still known as the Old Barrington Road. Barrington Ferry, important ferry since Colonial Days, was in use until the early years of the Twentieth Century.

(Located on GA 57, 3.7 miles north of Townsend. GHM 095-2, 1954.)

INDEX